D0463037

AFRICAN AMERICAN MILITARY HEROES

✦

BLACK ✦ STARS

AFRICAN AMERICAN MILITARY HEROES

JIM HASKINS

John Wiley & Sons, Inc.
New York • Chichester • Weinheim • Brisbane • Singapore • Toronto

Copyright © 1998 by Jim Haskins. All rights reserved.
Published by John Wiley & Sons, Inc.
Published simultaneously in Canada.

Design and production by Navta Associates, Inc.

This publication is designed to provide accurate and authoritative information in
regard to the subject matter covered. It is sold with the understanding that the pub-
lisher is not engaged in rendering professional services. If professional advice or
other expert assistance is required, the services of a competent professional person
should be sought.

Library of Congress Cataloging-in-Publication Data

Haskins, James.
     African American military heroes / by Jim Haskins.
         p. cm.—(Black stars series)
     ISBN 0-471-14577-7 (cloth : alk. paper)
         1. Afro-American soldiers—Biography—Juvenile literature.
     2. United States—Armed Forces—Afro-American troops—Juvenile literature.
3. United States—History, Military—Juvenile literature.   I. Title   II. Series.
E181.H35 1998
355'.008996073—dc21   98–14312

Printed in the United States of America
10 9 8 7 6 5 4 3 2 1

To Margaret Emily

CONTENTS

ACKNOWLEDGMENTS

I am grateful to Kathy Benson for her help. I would also like to thank the Institute of Texan Cultures, the U.S. Navy Department of Public Information, and the Women's Army Corps Museum.

INTRODUCTION

✦

Throughout American history, most African Americans have been eager to participate equally in society, and that has included defending their country. Despite centuries of being shut out from full participation in the rights of citizenship, blacks have loyally served their country in uniform in every major war.

During the Revolutionary War, 5,000 free blacks joined the Continental army. They often fought side by side with whites. But when the war was over, the new Congress of the United States barred blacks from joining state militias. Neither the navy nor the marines would let blacks enlist.

An era of exclusion had begun. Several hundred black sailors saw action in the War of 1812 against the British, but between the War of 1812 and the start of the Civil War in 1861, few blacks served in the military. The southern states that dominated the nation's military believed in rigid segregation. Northern states also placed many restrictions on blacks. Only a handful served in the conflict between the United States and Mexico (1846–1848), known as the Mexican War.

From 1850 until the Civil War, the peacetime army and navy were exclusively white.

When the Civil War broke out in 1861, African Americans rushed to take part. But even though the fight was largely about slavery, the Union forces would not admit them. That changed after President Abraham Lincoln issued the Emancipation Proclamation freeing slaves in the South. The Union needed black manpower to win. Before the war was over, nearly 180,000 black men—and at least one black woman in disguise—served in the Union army and navy, and nearly 40,000 died for the cause.

Reconstruction followed the Union victory in 1865. Congress passed civil rights acts and amendments to the United States Constitution guaranteeing blacks full citizenship. That included the right to serve in the military, although African Americans were restricted mainly to cavalry and infantry regiments on the western frontier. Nicknamed "Buffalo Soldiers" by the Indians, they patrolled the frontier and skirmished with the Indians. Black units also fought in the Spanish-American War (1898).

The United States declared war on Germany in 1917. Almost 400,000 African Americans enlisted or were drafted. More than 10 percent of American servicemen were black. But most worked in labor and stevedore battalions. In France, black troops under French commanders fought bravely and were well respected. But white American officers hated and scorned black troops under their command. The U.S. Army banned blacks from its combat divisions—the air, artillery, engineers, signal, and tank corps. The navy and marines excluded African Americans from all service except that of messmen in the kitchen.

In spite of continuing discrimination, a million African Americans joined the military when the United States entered World War II (1941–1945). Many saw combat and distinguished themselves for their courage and fighting ability. The army formed African American units. The Army Air Corps trained 1,000 black pilots, the famous

Tuskegee Airmen. Almost 4,000 black women served in the Women's Army Corps. Although the navy allowed blacks to serve only as messmen, three blacks won the Navy Cross, the navy's highest military honor. But segregation began to break down when there were not enough white men available to fight and the United States once again needed blacks in regular units.

A quiet revolution occurred after the war. In July 1948, President Harry S. Truman signed Executive Order 9981, which called for equality for all persons in the armed services. The new Department of the Air Force was the quickest to respond. At last, the army began to integrate. Many African Americans enlisted to fight in the Korean War (1950–1953). By the fall of 1954, integration in the military was complete.

In the spring of 1954, the United States Supreme Court handed down a watershed decision in the history of race relations. *Brown* v. *Board of Education, Topeka,* declared separate-but-equal schools unconstitutional. The decision triggered violence and conflict. Integration elsewhere in America would not be as peaceful as it had been in the military.

The Vietnam War (1954–1975) was the first war in U.S. history where blacks served in every type of military unit and fought in every major battle on land, on sea, and in the air. Today, in the words of General Colin Powell, the armed forces have become "the most democratic institution in America, where [you] rise or fall on merit."[1]

The people profiled in this book are only a few of the many courageous and dedicated African Americans who have beaten the odds and succeeded in their quest to defend our country. The actual number could fill many more such collections.

PART ONE

✦

THE
EARLY YEARS

PRIVATE PETER
SALEM

(1750–1816)

The 5,000 African Americans who served in the Revolutionary War had good reason to fight—they got their freedom when they enlisted in the Continental army. Among them was Peter Salem, who was also called Salem Middleux. Born a slave in Framingham, Massachusetts, he belonged, according to some sources, to Captain Jeremiah Belknap. Belknap sold him to Major Lawson of Buckminster, Massachusetts, a town near Boston.

In 1775, the American colonists' Continental army prepared to face the British occupying troops. The people of Boston readied for battle, and so did Peter Salem. He enlisted in the First Massachusetts Regiment as a private in Captain Simon Edgel's company and was granted his freedom.

Salem was at the April 1775 Battle of Lexington, against British Major John Pitcairn. He was also at Concord. Those battles marked the beginning of the Revolutionary War. On June 17, 1775, the colonists and British redcoats squared off at Bunker Hill. More than twenty-five blacks were in the colonial ranks. Private Peter Salem was among

them—as a servant to Lieutenant Grosvenor, who was facing Major Pitcairn a second time.

As the British advanced, colonial officers rode back and forth among the troops. "Don't fire 'til you see the whites of their eyes!" they urged. Peter Salem obeyed orders as long as he could. The king's soldiers charged a third time. Leading the charge, Major Pitcairn called out, "The day is ours!" Then a bullet from Private Peter Salem's gun shot him through. The colonists eventually drove the British from the hill and showed their enemy that they were a force to be reckoned with.

Although some observers said that several bullets brought Major Pitcairn down, most regarded Peter Salem as the hero. According to one report, they took up a collection to send Salem to General George Washington as the man who had slain Pitcairn.

The artist John Trumbull witnessed the battle from Roxbury, across the harbor from Bunker Hill, and possibly met Salem within the next few days. Trumbull painted the climactic scene ten years later, in London. He worked from memory and probably used a black model in his studio to represent Peter Salem. In the lower right section of the painting, Salem stands close behind Lieutenant Grosvenor, holding a French Charleville musket of the sort that fired the fatal bullet into Pitcairn.

Salem stayed with the Continental army, participating in the critical Battle of Saratoga in 1777, among others. With the American victory over the British in 1783, Salem left the army. That same year he married Katie Benson and settled in Leicester, Massachusetts, as a basket weaver. Eventually, he returned to Framingham, where he died in the town's poorhouse on August 16, 1816.

For some years after the Revolutionary War, engravings based on John Trumbull's painting included Peter Salem in a prominent position. But by 1855, according to William C. Nell, a black historian of the time, Salem was less visible: "In more recent editions, his figure is *non est inventus*. A significant but inglorious omission."[1]

THE FIRST HERO

Long before the first shots at Lexington and Concord, bands of colonists openly defied the redcoats, as the British soldiers were known. Crispus Attucks, the son of an African and a Native American, was the first patriot killed in one of those protests. He had been born a slave in 1723 in Framingham, Massachusetts, Peter Salem's birthplace. As a boy, he ran away to become a sailor. Attucks learned to read and write, and he grew devoted to the cause of freedom. Meeting with other protesters near the Boston courthouse on March 5, 1770, he died when British soldiers fired their muskets into the crowd. The incident became known as the Boston Massacre. A monument on Boston Commons honors Attucks's memory.

In 1882, the citizens of Framingham built a monument to the memory of Peter Salem. For many years, the Freedman's Bank of Boston printed his picture on their banknotes. The Daughters of the American Revolution bought Salem's home in 1909 and turned it into a historic site. In 1968, the federal government made a commemorative stamp of the Trumbull painting that included Peter Salem.

PRIVATE AUSTIN
DABNEY

(?-?)

Peter Salem had voluntarily enlisted in the Continental army, but Austin Dabney was sent in his master's stead. Born a slave in North Carolina, the son of a slave woman and her master, Dabney was owned by a Georgia colonist named Aycock. At the time, a colonist who did not wish to serve in the army could send a slave or servant in his place. Aycock sent Austin Dabney.

Dabney served as an artilleryman in the Battle of Battle Creek, Georgia. On February 4, 1779, a musket ball ripped through his thigh. Left on the battleground, he was found by a white soldier named Harris, who took him home and cared for him until he recovered. According to legend, Dabney never forgot Harris's kindness and

✦ An **artilleryman** fires the cannons or other large, mounted guns that are too heavy to be easily carried.

served the family faithfully for years afterward. Much later, the Harris family's eldest son found a way to thank Dabney for his loyalty and self-sacrifice.

When the Harris family moved to Madison County, Georgia, Dabney went with them. His hard work and saving made it possible for the eldest Harris son to go to Franklin College. When young Harris got a job in the office of state legislator Stephen Upson, he sought Upson's help for Dabney. Upson persuaded the Georgia Assembly to award Dabney a pension for his service in the Revolutionary War.

In 1819, the government held a lottery for land. It was only for Revolutionary War veterans. Although a pensioner, Dabney was not allowed in the lottery because he was black. After protests from Harris and others, the Georgia Assembly cited Dabney's "bravery and fortitude" in "several engagements and actions," and passed an act awarding Dabney 112 acres of land in Walton County, Georgia.[1] But a group of whites in Madison County protested the award, claiming "it was an indignity to white men, for a mulatto to be put upon an equality with them in the distribution of the public lands."[2]

To collect his pension, Dabney traveled once a year to Savannah. On one occasion he encountered the governor of Georgia, who recognized him and invited him into his home as an honored guest. Dabney prospered. He owned fine horses and attended races and bet on horses. But when the young Harris moved away from Madison County, Dabney went with him. Dabney died in Zebulon, Georgia.

Another African American patriot, James Armistead, became an undercover agent for the Continental army. For his service, he received this commendation from the Marquis de Lafayette.

PRIVATE LEMUEL
HAYNES

(1753–1833)

"**W**hen I was five months old, I was carried to Granville, Massachusetts, to be a servant to Deacon David Rose till I was Twenty-one. He was a man of singular piety. I was taught the principles of religion,"[1] recalled Lemuel Haynes about his life before the Revolutionary War. His mother was a white woman, and his father was a black man whom he never knew. Born on July 18, 1753, in West Hartford, Connecticut, Haynes was given up as a baby. On just one occasion later, Haynes met his mother by accident. She pretended not to know him, and he furiously reproached her. Even as a child, he had a strong sense of right and wrong.

The Roses were farmers, and young Lemuel helped them clear land and plant crops. There was little time left over for school. When he did go, he attended a common school with white children. He loved reading and spent his evenings poring over the Bible and books of psalms by the light of the fire. As he grew older, he read to the Rose family in the evenings.

One night, he slipped a sermon he had written into the book and read it to the family. Deacon David Rose was impressed. Since the parish had no minister, Rose asked his young servant to conduct the service and read an approved sermon, sometimes written by Lemuel.

By 1774, war clouds were gathering on the horizon of the British colonies in North America. Haynes stood up for his belief in what was right and joined the Minute Men, the colonial militia established by the Massachusetts provincial congress. Every week, he and his comrades practiced for battle in case they were needed. Soon enough, they were. After the Battle of Lexington, Massachusetts, in April 1775, Haynes accompanied Captain Lebbeus Ball's militia company to join the Continental army at Roxbury, Massachusetts. In 1776, Haynes marched in the expedition to Fort Ticonderoga, where with Ethan Allen and the Green Mountain Boys he helped to take the fort from British General Burgoyne's army.

✦A **militia** is a group of citizens legally called for military duty, but not part of the regular army.

Forty years later, in a sermon delivered on George Washington's birthday, Haynes would remind his listeners of his service in the Revolution: "Perhaps it is not ostentatious in the speaker to observe, that in early life he devoted all for the sake of freedom and independence, and endured frequent campaigns in their defence. . . ."[2]

Returning home from the war, Haynes put down his gun and took up the Bible again. In 1779, a clergyman in New Canaan, Connecticut, helped him learn Latin. Another supporter got him a teaching job and tutored him in Greek. Now Haynes could read the New Testament as originally written.

On November 29, 1780, after taking an examination in languages, sciences, and the gospel, Haynes became a preacher. A Congregational church in Middle Granville invited him to be its pastor, and he served that church for several years.

While in Granville, Haynes married Elizabeth Babbitt, a white former schoolteacher. They had ten children—seven girls and three boys.

In 1785, Haynes was officially ordained a minister of the gospel by an association of ministers in Litchfield, Connecticut. That same year, he accepted a position as pastor at a church in Torrington, Connecticut, becoming the first black pastor of a white church in the United States. One parishioner deliberately kept his hat on in church as a sign of disrespect. When the self-confident Reverend Haynes approached the pulpit, he either did not see or did not pay attention to the slight but began preaching. According to Haynes's biographer, Timothy Cooley, the parishioner later recalled, "My hat was instantly taken off and thrown under the seat, and I found myself listening with the most profound attention."[3]

But others did not come around, and the snubs of a determined clique in the congregation forced Haynes to leave Torrington after two years.

In March 1788, Haynes accepted a pastorship with a church in Rutland, Vermont, where he remained for thirty years. He was active in political and church circles throughout New England, speaking out on the moral wrong of slavery.

"I am pointing you to the poor Africans among us," he wrote in 1801. "What has reduced them to their present pitiful, abject state? Is it any distinction that the god of nature hath made in their formation? Nay—but being subjected to slavery, by the cruel hands of oppressors, they have been taught to view themselves as a rank of beings far below others, which has suppressed in a degree, every principle of manhood, and so they become despised, ignorant, and licentious. This should fill us with the utmost detestation against every attack on the rights of men. . . ."[4]

In 1804, Haynes was presented with a master of arts degree from Middlebury College in Vermont, thus becoming the first black person to receive an honorary degree from a white college in the United States.

Eventually, Haynes returned to Granville, Massachusetts. There, he spent the last eleven years of his life. He died on September 28, 1833, at the age of eighty.

Deborah
SAMPSON

(1760-1827)

At least one African American woman fought in the Revolutionary War, disguised as a man and able to keep her secret. Deborah Sampson wanted to be part of the events that affected her land, and she had the courage to do so.

Sampson was born on December 17, 1760, in Plymouth, Massachusetts, one of several children. Her father, Jonathan Sampson, was a sailor who disappeared at sea. Her mother, unable to care for the children, sent them to different families. Five-year-old Deborah lived first with a cousin, who died when Deborah was about eight. Then Deborah spent two years with the wife of a local pastor.

At the age of ten, Sampson was sent out as a servant to Benjamin Thomas of Middleborough, Massachusetts. For eight years, she not only did domestic chores, but she also worked in the fields, cared for the farm animals, and did carpentry. In addition, she managed to attend the local public school part-time. The Thomas children taught her what they knew. An avid reader, she was especially fond of newspapers and studied the major issues of the day.

Sampson was just thirteen years old at the time of the Boston Tea Party in 1773, the first major rebellion by American colonials against Great Britain. When the colonies declared their independence and the Revolutionary War began, she could not get enough of the news.

When Sampson was eighteen years old, her bondage to the Thomas family ended. She taught for six months at the same public school that she had attended. How she made her living after that is not known. In November 1780, she joined the First Baptist Church of Middleborough, but soon encountered problems. Accused of dressing in male clothing and engaging in conduct unbecoming a respectable lady, she was banished by the congregation.[1]

Sampson chafed against the restrictions of life in that Massachusetts town when such exciting events were taking place elsewhere. At some point, she determined to volunteer for the Continental army. Sampson was above average in height for a woman. Years of hard work for the Thomas family had made her strong. She purchased fabric and sewed a man's suit for herself. Then she walked to Billingham, Massachusetts. Using the alias Robert Shurtleff (or Shirtliff or Shirtlieff), she enlisted in the Continental army. Mustered into service at Worcester,

◆ To **muster** means to officially enroll someone in military service—or to discharge them.

Massachusetts, on May 23, 1782, she was assigned to Captain George Webb's company in the Fourth Massachusetts Regiment.

Sampson first served at White Plains, in the colony of New York, then moved with her company to Tarrytown, New York. In the battle at Tarrytown, she was wounded three times: a sword cut on the head and two musket balls in one leg.

At the Battle of Yorktown, Pennsylvania, four months later, Sampson was shot through the shoulder. During the march north after the battle, she succumbed to the extreme cold and other deprivations suffered by the soldiers of the Continental army and collapsed.

A DARING DECEPTION

Although Deborah Sampson was seriously wounded at Tarrytown, New York, she was afraid to go to a field hospital, because her true identity might be discovered. Despite her protests, her fellow soldiers carried her six miles to the nearest hospital.

There, Sampson reported only the head wound, which she knew she could not hide. She did not mention the two musket balls in her leg. While at the hospital, she somehow managed to get hold of surgical instruments and to remove one of the musket balls herself. The other was too deep to retrieve and remained in her leg. As soon as she had recovered sufficiently, she returned to her company.

Sampson was unconscious when she arrived at the field hospital operated by Dr. Barnabas Binney, a Philadelphia physician. In fact, it was first thought that she was dead. But Dr. Binney discerned a pulse, and in the course of treating her, he discovered that she was a woman. He kept this knowledge to himself, and when she was well enough to leave the hospital, he arranged for her to recuperate in his own home.

Formally and honorably discharged from the army by General Henry Knox at West Point on October 23, 1783, Sampson returned to New England and went to live with an uncle in Sharon, Massachusetts. There, she seems to have had no problems fitting into the community. She married a farmer named Benjamin Gannett on April 7, 1784. The couple had three children, a boy and two girls. They adopted another girl whose mother had died.

Sampson was proud of her service in the Continental army and, after her discharge, never tried to hide the truth of her daring deception. She sought, and was successful in securing, a government pension for her service. This event attracted the attention of Henry Mann, who became fascinated with her story and wrote a highly romanticized biography of Sampson, which was published in 1797. Mann also helped Sampson write a lecture about her experiences, which she first delivered at the Federal Street Theater in Boston on March 22, 1802. Thereafter, she lectured as often as she could, for her fees helped the family, who were not doing well at farming.

Sampson died on April 29, 1827, and was buried in Rockridge Cemetery in Sharon, Massachusetts. Carved on the back of her tombstone were these words: "Deborah Sampson Gannett, Robert Shurtleff, The Female Soldier: 1781–1783."

Several years later, her husband, Benjamin Gannett, petitioned Congress to collect his late wife's pension. Gannett argued that caring for her during her long and protracted illnesses resulting from her wounds in the Revolutionary War had left him in severe economic distress. In 1837, Congress granted Gannett a pension of $80 a year for the rest of his life.

A LETTER FROM PAUL REVERE

The Revolutionary War hero Paul Revere wrote a letter of support when Sampson applied for a federal government pension:

"This extraordinary woman is now in her 62d year of her age; she possesses a clear understanding, and a general knowledge of passing events; fluent in speech, and delivers her sentiment in correct language, with deliberate and measured accent; easy in deportment, affable in manners, robust . . .

"There are many living witnesses in this county, who recognized her on her appearance at the court, and were ready to attest to her services."[2]

VASHON

(1 7 9 2 – 1 8 5 4)

The Revolutionary War ended with the signing of the Treaty of 1783. Yet U.S. troubles with Great Britain continued, especially on the high seas. Embroiled in the Napoleonic Wars, Britain had a great need for sea power. It had the ships but often had difficulty finding the crews. To man its ships, Britain resorted to pressing deserters and criminals into service. British subjects who had adopted America as their country were also pressed into service, for at

> ✦ You are **pressed** into military service if you are forced to join.

that time England did not recognize the right of a person to change his or her nationality. British naval captains often used the search for British subjects as an excuse to intercept American ships. Once they had succeeded in boarding an American ship, they and their officers were none too careful about whom they took away. American resentment over British impressment of its citizens was one of the causes of the War of 1812.

The War of 1812 was primarily a naval war, and since the U.S. Navy admitted very few blacks at the time, blacks had little opportu-

nity to serve their country during this conflict. But while small in number, blacks again contributed to America's defense.

John Bathan Vashon was among them. Vashon was born in Norfolk, Virginia, the son of a mulatto mother. His father was Captain George Vashon, a white man of French ancestry. George Vashon was an Indian agent under General George Washington and later under President Martin Van Buren.

Like his father, John Vashon had set out as a young man looking for great adventure. He was twenty years old when the War of 1812 began. One of the few blacks accepted into the United States Navy, Vashon enlisted as a seaman and embarked on the USS *Revenge*. The *Revenge* was sailing off the coast of Brazil when it was engaged in battle by a British ship. The British force proved to be superior and took Vashon and other members of the crew of the *Revenge* prisoner. Luckily, they were later released in a prisoner exchange.

Discharged from the navy after the war ended in 1815, Vashon returned to Virginia, married, and started a family. Around 1822, he moved to Carlisle, Pennsylvania, where he ran a saloon for seven years. He then moved to Pittsburgh, where he became active in the anti-slavery movement. Vashon had found another worthy crusade.

Joining forces with the white abolitionist William Lloyd Garrison, Vashon participated in the growing campaign against slavery. He become a member of the Temperance and Moral Reform societies. He also helped organize and served as one of the vice presidents of the National Convention of Colored Men in Rochester, New York, in July 1853.

Vashon stayed in touch with other veterans of the War of 1812. Ironically, he was attending a convention of 1812 war veterans in Philadelphia when he had a heart attack and died on January 8, 1854.

WILLIAM
GOYENS

(1794-1856)

By the War of 1812, many people in the United States had begun to move westward to settle in the open territories. Frequently, they headed to Texas. In those days, Texas was part of Mexico, and Mexico was part of the Spanish empire. Mexico welcomed the newcomers to Texas. After all, they helped secure the frontier against the Indians. For little or no money, the Americans could obtain land for themselves from Mexico. All they had to do was convert to Catholicism, the official religion.

Unlike in the U.S. territories, slavery was outlawed in Texas. A Spanish census in 1792 found this interesting fact: Among the 1,600 residents of Texas were 263 black males and 186 black females. Probably, many of them were escaped slaves.[1]

Born a slave in South Carolina, William Goyens escaped to Texas in 1821, arriving via Galveston. He settled in Nacogdoches, and opened a blacksmith shop, using skills he had probably acquired as a slave in South Carolina.

By 1832, Goyens had married a woman from Georgia and prospered. In addition to his blacksmith business, he manufactured wagons and hauled freight. He also bought and sold land and racehorses. To improve his businesses, Goyens learned Spanish and several Indian dialects. The Mexican government of Texas appointed him an Indian agent to negotiate with the Cherokees.

During the Texas Revolution, Goyens served a similar function, negotiating with the Indians on behalf of the Americans in the Texans' fight for independence from Mexico.

After the successful revolt against Mexico, however, the newly independent Texas government made slavery legal and denied admittance to free blacks. This was especially unfair to the blacks who had answered Stephen Austin's call to arms (see box below). For example, a black citizen named Greenbury Logan fought with other Americans at Bexar, receiving wounds that left him permanently crippled. After the revolution, Greenbury Logan, unable to work his land or pay his taxes, lost the very rights that he had fought for.

THE CALL TO ARMS

Goyens came to Texas just as tensions were beginning to grow between the Mexican government and the rising number of U.S. settlers. By 1835, armed conflict broke out between these settlers and the Mexican forces.

When Stephen Austin, who more than anyone else had encouraged U.S. settlement in Texas, issued a call to arms, black settlers were among those who answered, and acknowledged Austin as their leader in the Texas Revolution.

William Goyens served in an important capacity. Austin's general, Samuel Houston, hired Goyens as his interpreter to negotiate a treaty with the Comanche Indians. He needed Goyens's skill with their language. Goyens successfully negotiated peace with the Comanche on behalf of the U.S. settlers.

Goyens was spared such indignities. In fact, the Texas Congress granted him a 2,000-acre tract of land west of Nacogdoches that came to be known as Goyens Hill. He raised cattle and horses and bought and sold land. In 1841, according to property records, Goyens owned 4,160 acres of improved land worth $20,600, two town lots, fifty head of cattle, two work horses, and other property.

Remembered for his charity as well as his wealth and good business sense, William Goyens died at his home on Goyens Hill on June 20, 1856, at the age of 62. A state centennial marker adorns his grave.

PART TWO

THE CIVIL WAR YEARS AND RECONSTRUCTION

Major Martin Robison
DELANY

(1812–1885)

For a quarter century after the Mexican War (1846–1848), the United States benefited from international peace. It expanded westward. New territories, including Texas, became states. The southern plantations prospered, finding huge markets for their cotton in Europe. Northern manufacturing grew steadily. It seemed that people everywhere wanted U.S.-manufactured products.

But while prosperous, the United States were far from peaceful. Slavery was causing deep divisions between northern and southern states, and this and other issues led to civil war.

For the first year and a half of the war, blacks waged their own struggle to get into the fight. Among those who fought most forcefully for the right to defend the Union was a physician named Martin Robison Delany, who became a major in the Union army.

Born of a free mother and a slave father in Charlestown, Virginia, on May 6, 1812, Delany learned early to be proud. His father, the son of an African chief, managed to gain his freedom. Seeking education for their children, the family moved to western Pennsylvania. Delany

ONE CAUSE OF THE CIVIL WAR

During the 1820s, the movement to abolish slavery grew in the North. One northern state after another outlawed slavery. In Congress, representatives from these states fought to admit new territories as states only if they, too, outlawed slavery. But southern representatives in Congress were just as determined that new states would be slave states. In contested territories like Kansas, armed conflict broke out between pro- and anti-slavery forces.

In 1860, the nation was like a tinderbox, ready to catch fire. The election of Republican Abraham Lincoln, who was not an abolitionist but who worried pro-slavery forces, provided the spark. It ignited armed rebellion. In 1861, seven southern states seceded from the Union and formed a new nation, the Confederate States of America. The federal government was determined to preserve the Union. The Civil War was on.

attended schools in Pittsburgh. He studied nights at a black church while also working during the day. He received medical training from two local physicians. When he moved for a time to the Southwest in the late 1830s, he worked as a physician's assistant and dentist. Years later, Delany decided to pursue formal medical studies. He was one of the first blacks admitted to Harvard Medical School. He did not graduate, however, because his fellow students petitioned successfully for his dismissal. After leaving Harvard, Delany returned to Pittsburgh, where he became a prominent physician as well as a leader of the black community.

Delany despaired that even whites who favored abolition would never accept blacks as equals. So he broke with Frederick Douglass and other abolitionists who believed blacks could be integrated into American society, and began to give serious thought to the idea of blacks leaving the United States. Perhaps they could seek a life of peace and equality elsewhere. At first, he advocated emigration to

Haiti or Central America, later to Africa. In 1854, he organized a National Emigration Convention of 100 men and women—the first women to be accepted as delegates to a black convention.

In 1856, in protest against oppressive conditions for blacks in the United States, Delany moved to Canada, where he continued his medical practice. In 1858, he presided over an emigration convention in Chatham, Canada. The convention appointed Delany as chief commissioner of a Niger River exploring party. Accompanied by Robert Campbell, a young schoolteacher from Philadelphia, Delany spent nine months in Africa, exploring the Niger River delta region. He made an agreement with the rulers of Ahbeokuta, in present-day Nigeria, for an African American settlement there. For his leadership of this expedition, and for his writings on black equality, Delany became known as the Father of Black Nationalism.

In 1861, Delany returned to the United States and joined Douglass and others urging President Lincoln to enlist blacks to fight in the

THE ABOLITIONIST

In Pittsburgh, Martin Delany started a weekly newspaper, *The Mystery*. He published it from 1843 to 1846. In its pages, he championed equal rights for both blacks and women. He also worked to move fugitive slaves north and to restore the vote to blacks in Pennsylvania.

Through his work, Martin Delany became friendly with the noted abolitionist Frederick Douglass. Even the great Douglass noticed Delany's fierce black pride. Douglass said, "I thank God for making me a man simply, but Delany always thanks Him for making him a black man."[1]

In 1847, Douglass invited Delany to be an editor of Douglass's weekly newspaper, *North Star,* published in Rochester, New York. Delany was listed on the masthead as an editor until 1849.

At the start of the Civil War, African Americans numbered 4 million enslaved and 480,000 free. After emancipation, thousands of black men joined the Union forces, sometimes followed by their families.

Civil War. Meeting personally with Lincoln, Delany proposed an army of blacks commanded by blacks. At first, the president did not agree.

At last, in 1863, the War Department mustered the all-black Fifty-fourth Massachusetts Volunteer Regiment. Delany, among those most actively recruited, served as its surgeon.

In February 1865, Delany became the first black man to receive a regular army commission. Major Delany traveled to Hilton Head Island, South Carolina, to recruit and organize former slaves for the North. But his efforts were cut short. The war ended in April with the surrender of Confederate General Robert E. Lee at Appomattox Court House, Virginia.

The federal government quickly sent occupying troops into the former Confederate states and established a period of Reconstruction, during which the Confederate states would write new constitutions. These would guarantee equal rights to the former slaves when the southern states were readmitted to the Union. The government also established a Freedmen's Bureau to help the former slaves. Delany served on the bureau in South Carolina.

In July 1865, Major Delany delivered a fiery speech to freedmen at the Brick Church, St. Helena Island. According to the army officer who reported on it, Delany said, "I want to tell you one thing. Do you know that if it wasn't for the black man, this war never would have been brought to a close with success to the Union, and the liberty of your race if it had not been for the Negro? I want you to understand that . . . they can't get along without you. Yankees from the north who come down here to drive you as much as ever it [was] before the war. It's slavery over again—northern, universal U.S. slavery."[2]

Delany urged his audience to be careful of trusting Yankees, to deal only with genuine government agents. He promised them that he would do all he could to work with the officers of the federal troops to see that the former slaves received their own plots of land to farm.

After an honorable discharge, Delany served with the Freedmen's Bureau in South Carolina for three more years. In 1874, he ran unsuccessfully as an Independent Republican for the office of lieutenant governor of South Carolina. He later became a customs inspector and trial justice in Charleston.

In his later years, Delany continued his scientific studies, publishing *Principia of Ethnology: The Origin of Race and Color* in 1879. He also published a novel, *Blake.* Among the lines he penned during his lifetime were these: "Fleecy locks and black complexions cannot alter nature's claim/ Skins may differ, but afflictions dwell in black and white the same."[3]

Major Delany died in Xenia, Ohio, on January 24, 1885.

LIEUTENANT PETER
VOGELSANG

(1815–1887)

Like Martin Delany, Peter Vogelsang became a commissioned officer in the all-black Fifty-fourth Massachusetts Volunteer Regiment. Born on August 21, 1815, in New York City, Vogelsang was working as a clerk when the Civil War broke out in April 1861.

At age forty-eight, Peter Vogelsang was by far the oldest recruit in the Fifty-fourth. Steady and serious, he soon became a father figure, particularly in Company H, one of the ten units into which the men were organized.

Vogelsang would have made a good commissioned officer from the start. But the army was firmly against the recruits becoming officers. Governor Andrew of Massachusetts wrote to Secretary of War Stanton, asking for colored officers such as surgeons and a chaplain to be placed in colored regiments. But both Stanton and President Lincoln feared that appointing black officers would outrage whites. The average white Northerner was against slavery in principle, but had no interest in blacks having equal rights of citizenship.

RECRUITING THE FIFTY-FOURTH

No one could keep the determined African Americans out of the war. Leading abolitionists like Martin Delany and Frederick Douglass continually pressed the cause. Escaped slaves made their way to Union lines and freedom. Union generals on the battlefields of the South found themselves suddenly responsible for the fugitives.

The Emancipation Proclamation turned the tide. It freed all slaves in the enemy states as of January 1, 1863. It declared that freed slaves "of suitable condition" would be "received into the armed service of the United States, to garrison forts, positions, stations, and other places, and to man vessels of all sorts."

Lincoln also agreed to enlist free blacks. Secretary of War Edwin M. Stanton authorized Governor John A. Andrew of Massachusetts to recruit and organize black soldiers into a regiment.

There was no question but that a white officer would command the first black regiment. Governor Andrew had just the officer in mind: Captain Robert Gould Shaw, Virginia-born son of abolitionists who had commanded the Second Massachusetts Infantry Regiment. Although Shaw expected ridicule for commanding a black regiment, he accepted Andrew's offer and a promotion to colonel.

Abolitionists rushed to recruit for the new regiment. Frederick Douglass recruited his own sons—Charles, nineteen, and Lewis, twenty-two. Robert Gould Shaw's father recruited Peter Vogelsang. The one thousand men who eventually comprised the regiment came from twenty-two states, the District of Columbia, and the West Indies. The majority were in their twenties.

When the Fifty-fourth was mustered into service in March 1863, all twenty-nine officers were white. Colonel Robert Gould Shaw reported to General David Hunter in Hilton Head, South Carolina.

Barely had the Fifty-fourth made camp when Colonel James Montgomery ordered company H and seven others to travel further south to Darien, Georgia. They watched as Union gunboats fired on the town. Then Montgomery ordered them to plunder and torch the houses. It was more like piracy than warfare. Shaw protested, but Montgomery was determined to destroy the town. The men of the Fifty-fourth reluctantly followed their orders.

Shaw promoted Peter Vogelsang almost as soon as the Fifty-fourth Massachusetts reached the South. He rose to sergeant first, and then, on April 17, to quartermaster sergeant, both noncommissioned ranks. Ordinarily, that would have meant a raise in pay. But the Fifty-fourth Massachusetts did not operate under ordinary circumstances.

✦ A **noncommissioned** officer (for example, a sergeant) is appointed from among the enlisted soldiers. He or she reports to a commissioned officer (for example, a captain).

✦ A **column** is a formation of troops, one behind the other.

In early July, the Fifty-fourth Massachusetts joined other Union regiments in a campaign against Charleston, South Carolina. The regiment sailed north on the steamer *Chasseur*. On July 11, Vogelsang and

EQUAL PAY—A MATTER OF PRIDE

On June 30, the Fifty-fourth was mustered for pay for the first time. Instead of a soldier's $13 plus a clothing allowance, they got $10, the rate for laborers, minus $3 for clothing. Furious at this insult, they refused payment. Governor Andrew offered to make up the difference with money from the state treasury. But the men of the Fifty-fourth refused again. It was not the money but the principle involved. They believed that their federal government should pay them as much as white soldiers. Out of pride, they continued to refuse any pay at all for eighteen months, in spite of the hardships that decision imposed on their families. But they did not refuse to serve, although Shaw felt they should be released from duty if they were not to be treated equally with white troops.

his comrades debarked on James Island, off the coast of South Carolina, where several Confederate regiments waited. It was there that the Fifty-fourth Massachusetts came under fire for the first time.

It seemed to Sergeant Peter Vogelsang that all at once "one hundred Rebels were swarming about me."[1] He not only stood fast but advanced, taking with him his whole company. Although he was wounded, he still managed to accompany the Fifty-fourth to the battle that made it famous, the assault on Fort Wagner.

On July 16, 1863, the men of the Fifty-fourth were ordered to begin a forced march that lasted a day and a half. Their destination was Charleston, South Carolina, and their mission was to capture Fort Wagner, a Confederate stronghold guarding the entrance to Charleston Harbor. They had rested from their long march only about thirty minutes when Brigadier General George C. Strong, who had replaced Colonel Montgomery, gave the order for the charge. The column advanced. Immediately, the fort's big guns and muskets fired on them. Colonel Robert Gould Shaw was killed, but his men fought on. (See Sergeant William H. Carney's story on page 67.)

Although the Fifty-fourth failed to capture the fort, it proved its bravery. Northern newspapers made much of the battle and of the courage of the black troops. Union General Ulysses S. Grant, commander of all army forces, wrote to President Lincoln, "By arming the Negro we have added a powerful ally. They will make good soldiers and taking them from the enemy weakens him in the same proportion they strengthen us. I am therefore most decidedly in favor of pushing this policy to the enlistment of a force sufficient to hold all the South falling into our hands and to aid in capturing more."[2]

Congress awarded fourteen members of the Fifty-fourth Massachusetts the Medal of Honor, established during the Civil War as the highest military award for bravery, for their courageous assault on Fort Wagner. That battle changed the attitude of many Northerners toward the black volunteers.

The Fifty-fourth Massachusetts continued to see action until the war ended in April 1865. Peter Vogelsang rose to second lieutenant and then first lieutenant—one of only three men in the Fifty-fourth to be commissioned as officers. On August 20, 1865, his term of service expired, Lieutenant Vogelsang returned to New York City and lived another twenty years. He died on April 4, 1887.

HARRIET TUBMAN

(1820–1913)

Harriet Tubman, a fearless scout, spy, and nurse, was born on the plantation of Edward Brodas in Dorchester County, Maryland. Her parents, Harriet Greene and Benjamin Ross, were enslaved. When she was born, she was named Araminta; but later she was called Harriet, after her mother. When Harriet was six, her master hired her out to work for local people, who treated her cruelly. On the Brodas plantation, she received an injury that would cause her to suddenly lose consciousness at random times for the rest of her life. She had attempted to block the way of an overseer chasing after a slave who was trying to escape. A brick intended for the runaway hit her instead.

In 1848, Harriet married John Tubman, a freeman. When she confided in him that she wanted to escape, he threatened to report her. But when Harriet learned that she had been sold to a Georgia slave trader, she escaped and made her way to Philadelphia. After two years in Philadelphia, Harriet learned that her sister and children were about to be sold. She returned to Maryland to assist her sister's

husband in rescuing his family from a slave pen in Cambridge, Maryland. Not long after that daring rescue, she returned to the Brodas plantation. She wanted to persuade her husband to join her in the North. Instead, she found that he had remarried. Undaunted, Harriet brought out eleven slaves, including one of her brothers and his wife.

By 1851, she had become a legend as a conductor on the Underground Railroad, the network of people, black and white, who aided slaves escaping from the South to the North and freedom. She established a pattern that she kept to for six years, until 1857. Each year she made two trips to the South, one in the spring and one in the fall. She spent the winters in St. Catherine's, Ontario, where many fugitive slaves had settled, and the summers working in hotels in places such as Cape May, New Jersey, to earn money for her trips. In the spring of 1857, she managed to rescue her aged parents.

By the fall of 1858, Tubman had helped more than 300 slaves reach the North and freedom. She had come to be called Moses for leading her people to the promised land. By 1860, the reward for her capture was $40,000—a huge sum in those days. In December 1860, she made her last trip as a conductor on the Underground Railroad. By early 1861, the North and South were at war, and it was no longer possible to continue her trips south.

During the Civil War, Tubman served the Union cause in several ways. In May 1862, months before the first Northern black regiments were authorized, Tubman arrived in Beaufort, South Carolina. She had joined a group of missionary-teachers to aid the hundreds of escaped slaves who had made their way to Union lines after the Union fleet had captured the South Carolina sea islands. Tubman showed the women that by doing the soldiers' laundry, they could earn money and become self-supporting. Tubman personally built and financed a washhouse to get them started. She also nursed both soldiers and freedmen at the army hospital on the islands.

THE UNION SCOUT

Harriet Tubman aided numerous expeditions, the most famous in 1863. She accompanied guerrilla fighter Colonel James Montgomery and about 800 African American soldiers of the Second South Carolina Volunteers on a gunboat raid along the Combahee River in South Carolina. She and her scouts surveyed the area and identified places where Confederate soldiers had placed explosives along the river. With this crucial information, the Union gunboats zigzagged up the river, avoiding the explosives and picking off small bands of Confederate soldiers. Meanwhile, Union troops made their way along both riverbanks, setting fire to plantation fields, dwellings, and stores of cotton.

♦ A **guerrilla** is someone who fights undercover.

Confederate troops retreated, and plantation families fled with them, taking as many slaves as they could. Some plantation slaves saw their chance for freedom. They ran to the river from all directions, waving and shouting to the Union gunboats. The seamen took them aboard and back to Union camps. That expedition rescued more than 750 African Americans.

An army officer asked her to go to Fernandina, Florida, to treat soldiers suffering from dysentery. She cured many with a medicine she prepared from roots dug out of the marshes.

Tubman also recruited a group of former slaves as Union scouts. They hunted for Confederate camps. They reported on enemy troop movements and on the locations of cotton warehouses, ammunition depots, and slaves waiting to be liberated. Her years as an Underground Railroad conductor had taught her the back roads and forest paths of the upper South. She knew how to move around without being detected. She also knew how to play the role of the old, harmless freedwoman when it suited her.

After about two years of serving the Union, Tubman received word that her parents, old and in poor health, needed her attention. She traveled to Auburn, New York, where she had bought a home for

A NURSE REMEMBERS

Another African American woman who devoted herself to helping win the war was Susie King Taylor (1848–1912). Born a slave on a plantation near Savannah, Georgia, she joined the First South Carolina Volunteers. Starting out as a laundress, she accepted other tasks with enthusiasm. In her memoirs, *Reminiscences of My Life in Camp* (1902), she wrote:

"I learned to handle a musket very well and could shoot straight and often hit the target. I assisted in cleaning the guns and used to fire them off, to see if the cartridges were dry, before cleaning and reloading. . . . [After a battle] I hastened down to the landing when the wounded began to arrive, some with their legs off, arm gone, foot off, and wounds of all kinds imaginable.

"There are many people who do not know what colored women did during the war. Hundreds of them assisted Union soldiers by hiding them and helping them to escape. Many were punished for taking food to the prison stockades for the prisoners . . . although they knew what the penalty would be should they be caught."[1]

Susie King Taylor, the first known black army nurse in American history, served with the First Regiment of South Carolina during the Civil War.

them, and cared for them until she herself became ill. But Harriet was strong. Soon enough, she was back on her feet, working as matron of the Colored Hospital at Fortress Monroe.

After the war, Tubman tried, but failed, to secure a government pension for her service to the Union forces. So she started selling eggs and vegetables door-to-door. A neighbor helped her write her story, *Scenes from the Life of Harriet Tubman.* The book brought in a small income. In March 1869, she married Nelson Davis, more than twenty years her junior. He suffered from tuberculosis contracted during the war. Selfless as always, she cared for him until he died in 1888, at age forty-four. As his widow, she finally collected a military pension of $20 per month. She died on March 10, 1913.

GOVERNOR
PINCKNEY BENTON STEWART
PINCHBACK

(1837–1921)

Pinckney Benton Stewart Pinchback was born free on May 10, 1837, in Macon, Georgia. He was the eighth child of Eliza Stewart and Major William Pinchback, a white Mississippi planter. Eliza Stewart had been enslaved when her seven other children were born, but by the time of Pinckney's birth, she had been freed. When Pinckney and his older brother, Napoleon, were nine and sixteen respectively, their father sent them to Gilmore's School in Cincinnati. After eighteen months, they were called home. Major Pinchback was dying. On his death, his relatives back east seized his estate. Fearing that they might attempt to re-enslave her and her children, Eliza Stewart fled. She went to Cincinnati with her five youngest children—Napoleon, Mary, Pinckney, Adeline, and a baby girl.

Napoleon soon proved mentally unfit to work, so at the age of twelve Pinckney became the major support of his family. He signed on as a cabin boy on the canal boats running between Cincinnati and Miami, Toledo and Fort Wayne, at a salary of $8 a month. Hardworking and smart, he was eventually promoted to

P. B. S. PINCHBACK.
EX-GOVERNOR OF LOUISIANA.

steward. In 1860, he married Nina Emily Hawthorne, whom he had met in Memphis.

After the Confederates fired on Fort Sumter in 1861, Pinchback started looking for a way to get into the fight on the side of the Union. He found it in New Orleans, a cosmopolitan city with a large population of free blacks. Union navy admiral David Farragut had captured New Orleans in 1862. Soon after, Major General Benjamin J. Butler put out a call for a regiment of black soldiers, the Corps d'Afrique, for the Louisiana National Guard. Pinchback jumped at the chance to get into the military. He traveled to New Orleans, where he set about recruiting a company.

The enthusiastic twenty-four-year-old managed to raise an entire company in just over a week. The Second Louisiana Native Guards entered into service for the Union on October 12, 1862, under the command of Captain P. B. S. Pinchback.

What a contrast this was to the Union army in the North. For the first time, black troops could serve under their black officers. All three of the black regiments—the First, Second, and Third Louisiana Native

UNDER ENEMY FIRE

The black units saw their first combat during May and June of 1863. The long battle of Port Hudson, Louisiana, included two Louisiana Native Guard regiments and six Corps d'Afrique regiments. Officers, white and black, had stories to tell of the brave black soldiers.

Captain Pinchback's men incurred severe injuries, but rejoined the fray rather than go to a field hospital. With exceptional determination, they kept advancing when certain to be assaulted by enemy fire. Major General Banks reported on the black troops: "The severe test to which they were subjected, and the determined manner in which they encountered the enemy, leaves upon my mind no doubt of their ultimate success."[1]

Guards (unlike the other regiments, the latter was composed of former slaves)—had black officers.

The black regiments distinguished themselves in battle, but that did not affect the opinion of Major General Nathaniel Banks. Ironically, even after witnessing the valor of the black soldiers, Banks still disapproved of black officers in general. Pinchback and the other black officers learned that their commissions were merely temporary, pending qualification examinations. In the next few months, one by one they were disqualified and mustered out. Their places were taken by white officers. Of all the original black officers of the Corps d'Afrique, only Pinchback qualified.

Pinchback was determined to have the respect he deserved as a Union officer. He refused to ride on the New Orleans streetcars marked with a large star for "colored" passengers. Whenever he rode a streetcar, he rode alone—the car blocked off by streetcar personnel so that no white passenger could board. No direct action was taken against Pinchback. Instead, he was denied the opportunity to rise in the ranks of the Corps d'Afrique. Twice he was passed over for promotion.

By September 1863, Pinchback had had enough. He was much too proud to allow the situation to continue. He submitted his letter of resignation:

Fort Pike, Louisiana, September 10, 1863

General:

In the organization of the regiment I am attached to [Twentieth Corps d'Afrique] I find nearly all the officers inimical to me, and I can foresee nothing but dissatisfaction and discontent, which will make my position very disagreeable indeed. I would therefore, respectfully tender my resignation, as I am confident by so doing I best serve the interest of the regiment.

I have the honor to be, sir, very respectfully, your obedient servant.

P. B. S. Pinchback
Captain Second Class
Louisiana National Guard[2]

After the war, Pinchback entered politics in Louisiana. He was an able leader. A delegate to the state constitutional convention, his major achievement was the successful introduction of the Thirteenth Amendment to the state's constitution, guaranteeing civil rights to all people of the state. He was elected first to the state senate, then as its president *pro tem*. When the lieutenant governor died in 1871, Pinchback succeeded to that office. In early December 1872, Louisiana governor Henry Clay Warmoth was impeached, and Lieutenant Governor Pinchback succeeded him, serving as acting governor from December 9, 1872, to January 13, 1873. Those forty-two days made him the first African American governor of a state—and the only black to hold such a position until the election of L. Douglas Wilder as governor of Virginia in 1990.

In 1872, Pinchback was elected to the U.S. House of Representatives from Louisiana; but his Democratic opponent protested the election and won the seat. The following year, Pinchback was elected to the U.S. Senate, but again he was refused the seat. When Reconstruction ended in 1877, Pinchback's career in elective office ended, too. He earned a law degree from Straight University, New Orleans, and was admitted to the bar of federal and state courts in Louisiana in 1886. He moved with his family to Washington, D.C., and in 1890 organized an American Citizens' Equal Rights Association. Traveling throughout the South and Midwest, he formed local branches of the association.

Governor Pinchback died on December 21, 1921. Two of his and Nina's sons had died, as had their one daughter. Of the two sons who survived, the younger, Walter A., also had a military career. A graduate of Andover Academy and Howard University Law School, Walter Pinchback, a lieutenant in the U.S. Army, served in the infantry in the Spanish-American War.

CAPTAIN MICHAEL A.
HEALY

(1839–1904)

Michael A. Healy was born near Clinton, Georgia, on September 22, 1839. His father was Michael Morris Healy, an Irishman, who had come to Georgia from Canada in 1812. His mother was an enslaved African American. She was born on the cotton plantation owned by Sam Griswald, who was probably her father.

The Healys had ten children. Three became Catholic priests—one, the first black Catholic bishop; another, the first and only black president of Georgetown University in Washington, D.C. As enterprising as his brothers, young Michael had little interest in a religious career or in going to college. Instead, on March 7, 1865, shortly before the Civil War ended, he enlisted in the United States Revenue Cutter Service, the forerunner of the United States Coast Guard.

◆ A **cutter** is a small ship equipped with weapons.

Intelligent and able, Healy rose to second lieutenant by June 1866. He was named first lieutenant in 1870 and captain in 1883. He sailed mostly out of San Francisco to Alaska and the Arctic.

Among the ships Healy commanded were the *Chandler,* the *Bear,* and the *Corwin.* The *Bear* was particularly famous. In 1884, while part of the U.S. Navy fleet, she had rescued an expedition of explorers off the uncharted coast of Greenland. When the navy assigned the *Bear* to the U.S. Revenue Cutter Service, Captain Michael Healy was its first skipper.

Healy cared for the daily needs of the people of Alaska. It was his idea to import reindeer from Russia across the Bering Strait to provide food for the native Alaskans and hide for their clothing. He imported the first dozen reindeer in 1879. Over the next ten years, he helped bring in some 1,100 more.

When Captain Healy retired on September 22, 1903, he was the third-ranking captain in the U.S. Revenue Cutter Service. He died on August 30, 1904.

In the mid-1990s, the U.S. Coast Guard commissioned a new diesel electric ice-breaking ship able to carry a crew of seventy-five, plus thirty-five science personnel. It was christened the USCGC (United States Coast Guard Cutter) *Healy,* a fitting honor.

THE DEPUTY MARSHAL

The United States purchased Alaska from Russia in 1867 for a total of $7.2 million. The huge territory was the last earthly frontier of the United States. Its small population depended on the U.S. Revenue Cutter Service for mail and supplies and for legal authority.

For many years, Captain Healy protected the federal law in Alaska as a deputy marshal. One of the single most important people in the territory, he tracked down seal poachers and murderers. His unpredictable temper earned him the nickname Hell Roarin' Mike Healy.

CONGRESSMAN ROBERT
SMALLS

(1839–1915)

The majority of blacks who fought in the Civil War served in the Union army. Robert Smalls had the distinction of serving both the Confederacy and the Union at sea. But he did not voluntarily aid the Confederate cause.

Born in Beaufort County, South Carolina, Smalls had a Jewish father and a black mother. He learned sail-making and rigging from his father. After the Civil War broke out, Smalls was pressed into the Confederate service on the ship *Planter*. As pilot, Smalls ferried supplies and munitions from Charleston Harbor out to Fort Ripley and Fort Sumter, avoiding the Union blockade.

In the spring of 1862, Robert Smalls had a daring idea. He made up his mind to hijack the *Planter*. He planned to make a run for the Union blockade even though two Confederate officers guarded the black crew. Smalls and his brother John, the assistant pilot

> ✦ **Munitions,** or ammunition, are the explosive devices used by the military.
>
> ✦ A **blockade** uses troops or ships to prevent the enemy from transporting supplies or traveling.
>
> ✦ **Fortifications** are the structures built to defend a position.

on the *Planter,* enlisted the support of the other black crew members. One night when the officers went ashore, the black crew cast off from the dock at Charleston and slowly steamed down the harbor. As the *Planter* passed Fort Sumter, she fired her guns in salute. Since it was not unusual to see the ship traveling about in the early morning hours, she aroused no suspicion. The *Planter* managed to get by all the Confederate fortifications without any problem. The crew then raised a white flag signaling surrender and made their way at full steam toward the Union ships blockading the harbor entrance.

Fortunately for Smalls, the Union sailors saw the white flag just before they started to fire on *Planter.* Holding their fire, they were surprised to see only blacks aboard. Nearing the stern of the Union ship *Onward,* Robert Smalls stepped forward, took off his hat, and said, "Good morning, sir! I've brought you some of the old United States guns, sir!"[1]

The U.S. government offered prize money for any Confederate ship. Smalls and his crew received half the prize money for capturing the *Planter* and remained on the ship.

The navy had accepted black enlistees even before the Civil War, but there is no evidence that either Smalls or any of his crew actually saw service in the United States Navy. U.S. government records show that Smalls signed a contract to be master of the *Planter* for the Union from February to July 1865. There was always at least one white Union officer on board. It was against navy policy to place blacks in command. Smalls and his crew served for the remainder of the Civil War, once narrowly escaping recapture by the Confederates.

After the war, Smalls enlisted in the South Carolina National Guard, where he achieved the rank of major general. He was a delegate to the 1868 South Carolina Constitutional Convention. He then served two terms in the state legislature and two terms in the state senate. Smalls was among the sixteen African Americans who were elected to Congress during Reconstruction. He was elected to Congress in 1876, 1878, 1880, and 1882, serving longer than any other black congressman of the period. Congressman Smalls died in 1915.

SERGEANT MAJOR CHRISTIAN A.
FLEETWOOD

(c.1840–?)

Christian A. Fleetwood was born in Baltimore, Maryland, about 1840. Whether he was born free is not known, but he attended private schools. He went to Ashmund Institute, a new secondary school in Lincoln, Pennsylvania. The school later became Lincoln University, and Fleetwood was in the first graduating class in 1858. He seemed comfortably settled in free black society. As he wrote later, "I had already some reputation as a singer of some note for the sweetness and purity of tone."[1]

When the Civil War broke out, Fleetwood eagerly joined the Union army. "A double purpose induced me and most others to enlist, to assist in abolishing slavery and to save the country from ruin."[2] On August 11, 1863, he was assigned to army headquarters in Baltimore. Given the rank of sergeant major, he did bookkeeping. He kept the soldier's rosters and wrote reports.

Barely a month passed before Fleetwood's regiment headed out for Yorktown, Virginia. In less than a week, they were ordered on a raid. From then on, Fleetwood was in the thick of the war. There were raids

once or twice a month. After April 1864, he was in Point Lookout, Maryland, guarding Confederate prisoners. Then the army formed the United States Colored Troops.

Fleetwood's new, black regiment was the Third Division, Eighteenth Army Troops. They built defenses, fought to hold them, and made reconnaissances. On June 15, some 250 men in the Third Division died in battle at Petersburg, Virginia.

◆ A **roster,** in the military, is a list of the names of officers and men on active duty.

◆ A **reconnaissance** is done before a military attack to explore and survey the enemy territory.

◆ The **color bearer** is someone who carries the flag.

◆ The **colors** are a flag or badge.

They again faced heavy fire from enemy guns on September 29, 1864. At Chapin's Farm in New Market Heights, Virginia, under Major General William Birney, Fleetwood and his fellow soldiers lost two-thirds of their remaining force. Fleetwood saw the two color bearers shot down. He seized the colors and carried them for the rest of the battle. For his valor, he received the Medal of Honor on April 6, 1865.

Confederate General Robert E. Lee surrendered to Union General Ulysses S. Grant at Appomattox Court House, Virginia, on April 9,

WHY CONTINUE TO SERVE?

Dr. James Hall, Fleetwood's former employer, recognized his abilities and urged him to re-enlist. Writing to Hall on June 8, 1865, Fleetwood explained his reluctance:

"Upon all our record there is not a single blot, and yet no member of this regiment is considered deserving of a commission or if so cannot receive one. I trust you will understand that I speak not of and for myself individually or that the lack of the pay or honor of a commission induces me to quit the service. Not so by any means, but I see no good that will result to our people by continuing to serve. On the contrary it seems to me that our continuing to act in a subordinate capacity with no hope of advancement or promotion is an absolute injury to our cause."[3]

1865. Fleetwood performed garrison duty at Fort Slocum until May 1866. Then, like the vast majority of other African American soldiers, he was discharged from the army.

Soon after, Fleetwood helped found the Soldiers' and Sailors' League in Philadelphia, Pennsylvania. He settled in Washington, D.C., and became a respected citizen. For a time, he taught school. Then he worked with the Freedman's Bank. In 1881, he went to work in the War Department. Using War Department records, he wrote about black soldiers during the Revolutionary War.

Fleetwood joined the District of Columbia National Guard, serving as captain in the Independent Company from 1880 to 1887 and as major from 1887 to 1892.

In his old age, Fleetwood was deaf in the left ear from "gunshot concussion" and also in the right, a result of "disease contracted in the army." But he died of heart trouble.

When Sergeant Major Fleetwood died, the prominent Reconstruction politicians P. B. S. Pinchback and Henry Johnson were honorary pallbearers. So was Major Charles R. Douglass, one of Frederick Douglass's sons. Fleetwood had been a member of the Frederick Douglass Post, G.A.R. After the funeral at St. Thomas Episcopal Church, he was laid to rest in Harmony Cemetery near Washington, D.C.

Proud of going to war for the Union, soldiers such as Andrew Scott paused to have their portraits made.

SERGEANT WILLIAM H.
CARNEY

(c. 1840–1908)

The first African American to win the Congressional Medal of Honor, William H. Carney was born to an enslaved black woman and her free husband, a seaman, in Norfolk, Virginia. Carney and his mother were freed from slavery when he was fourteen years old.

When Carney was growing up, it was illegal to teach blacks to read in Virginia, as elsewhere in the South. Carney studied for a time at a school secretly operated by a minister. He also worked at sea with his father.

In 1856, Carney's family moved to New Bedford, Massachusetts, a whaling seaport. There, he joined a church and studied for the ministry. But when the Civil War broke out, and the Union army began to accept black enlistees, Carney signed up. In February 1863, Carney joined the Fifty-fourth Massachusetts Volunteer Regiment, the first African American regiment recruited by the United States Army, raised by Massachusetts Governor John A. Andrew.

The Fifty-fourth Massachusetts headed to South Carolina. On July 18, 1863, after a forced march that had lasted a day and a half, the

men of the Fifty-fourth faced Fort Wagner, a Confederate stronghold guarding the entrance to Charleston Harbor. They had

✦ An **assault** is a violent physical attack.

rested from their long march only about thirty minutes when they got the order to begin the assault on the fort.

Their column advanced. Immediately, they felt the fire from the fort's big guns as well as from muskets. Colonel Robert Gould Shaw, their commander, fell dead at the head of his regiment. His men fought on. Many of them reached the fort's walls and clambered over them, aiming to disable the big guns. But the musket fire increased. White regiments in the vicinity could have helped the Fifty-fourth, but for various reasons none were able to do so. Without support, the regiment finally had to retreat, having lost a third of its men.

The Fifty-fourth did not capture the fort. But they proved their bravery and their willingness to die for the Union cause. The survivors knew this truth. It took nearly thirty years for the government to acknowledge it.

For his valor on June 18, 1863, during the Battle of Fort Wagner, Carney was cited for the Congressional Medal of Honor. He did not receive the actual medal until May 23, 1900.

THE DETERMINED FLAG BEARER

In the thick of the fighting at Fort Wagner, Sergeant William H. Carney saw the bearer of the American flag fall. He grabbed the flag before it touched the ground. He planted it on the fort, taking Confederate bullets in each leg, one in the chest, and one in his right arm in the process. Just then the order came to retreat. Carney picked up the flag again and carried it safely back to the Union lines. "The old flag never touched the ground, boys," he proudly said later.[1]

After the war, the colors Carney carried were enshrined in the Massachusetts statehouse. Sargeant Carney was discharged from the army in 1864. He lived for two years in California, then returned to New Bedford, where he worked as a mail carrier until 1901. He retired that year and moved to Boston, where he worked as a messenger in the statehouse. He died on December 9, 1908.

Attacking Fort Wagner, the Fifty-fourth Massachusetts valiantly faces Confederate artillery.

SERGEANT GEORGE WASHINGTON
WILLIAMS

(1849–1891)

George Washington Williams fought not only in the Civil War but also in the Mexican War. Born on October 16, 1849, at Bedford Springs, Pennsylvania, Williams was the second child and firstborn son in his family. His mother, Ellen Rouse Williams, was of African and German heritage. His father, Thomas Williams, was of African and Welsh descent.

Thomas Williams was a minister and a barber. By 1860, he owned real estate valued at $500. He traveled a lot, and Ellen Rouse Williams went out to work, leaving young George pretty much on his own. George's education was scanty, but he knew that change was in the air. The Civil War was brewing.

In 1860, when he was only eleven, Williams wrote a letter to Union General O. O. Howard. In it, Williams said his "Hart Burned with Eager Joy to meet the Planter on the Field of Battle to prove our Human Cherater [character]."[1]

The war was in its fourth year in the summer of 1864, when, at the age of fifteen, Williams attempted to enlist. He was found to be too

young. He tried again—this time traveling to Meadville in northwestern Pennsylvania to do so. He lied about his age and registered as William Seward—or Charles Steward.

According to Williams's own account, he served for a while with the Tenth Army Corps, commanded by Major General D. B. Birney. Wounded in September 1864 in an assault on Fort Harrison, near Richmond, Virginia, Williams recovered quickly and returned to the fight. When all the black troops became the U.S. Colored Troops, Williams was assigned to the Second Division of the Twenty-fifth Army Corps. He saw action at Hatcher's Run, Five Forks, and along the 16-mile battle line to Petersburg, Virginia. When Petersburg fell on April 2, 1865, Williams was there. Soon after, the Confederates surrendered.

Back home in Pennsylvania, Williams probably realized that a young black man with no formal education and few skills also had few opportunities. Most of the black soldiers who had fought in the

"SOLDIER OF FORTUNE"

After the war, the Twenty-fifth Army Corps went to Texas, and shortly thereafter, George Washington Williams left the army. He may have been discharged because of his age or mustered out as expected. He may have deserted. The real reason is not known.

The adventurous teenager crossed the Texas border into Mexico. Mexican general Espinosa was fighting to overthrow Emperor Maximilian, an Austrian archduke who was ruling Mexico for France. The United States was on General Espinosa's side. Williams joined Espinosa's army against the French. But it is unlikely that Williams or any of the other American soldiers of fortune who fought against Maximilian really understood the politics. He received a commission as lieutenant and served until the spring of 1867. Just before the final march to victory over Maximilian, Williams returned to the United States.

Civil War had been mustered out, and the United States Army had taken few steps toward making a permanent place for African Americans.

Regardless, Williams went to Pittsburgh and enlisted for five more years in the Twenty-seventh Infantry, under the command of Captain H. Haymond. As a drill sergeant, Williams helped get 100 recruits and then delivered them to Fort Riley, Kansas. Assigned to the Indian Territory with the Tenth Calvary, Williams assisted in the rebuilding of Fort Arbuckle and in providing protection for settlers on the frontier. The Tenth Calvary also campaigned against the Comanches, but it is not known whether Williams actively participated. He received a gunshot wound to his lung on May 19, 1868, but not in the line of duty. Whatever the circumstances, he was hospitalized for the rest of his time in the army.

On September 4, 1868, Williams received a Certificate of Disability for Discharge. His military career was over, and he had not yet reached his nineteenth birthday.

Following his discharge, Williams began to study for the ministry, first in St. Louis, Missouri, then at Howard University in Washington, D.C. Finally, he enrolled at Newton Theological Institution (now Seminary), in Newton, Massachusetts. In 1874, he was the first black to graduate. That same year, he also married Sarah Sterrett of Chicago and was ordained a minister at Watertown, Massachusetts. For some years, he served as pastor of Twelfth Street Baptist Church in Boston. He and Sarah had one child before their divorce in 1886.

Ever restless, Williams moved to Washington, D.C., where he started a newspaper, *The Commoner.* He then moved to Cincinnati, Ohio, where he was named minister of Union Baptist Church and wrote for local publications. He started to read law, and he was admitted to the Ohio bar in 1879. That same year, he campaigned for and won election to the Ohio Legislature from Hamilton County, becoming the first black state legislator in Ohio.

While in Ohio, Williams developed a strong interest in African American history and became a voracious reader. In 1883, he published a two-volume, 1,000-page *History of the Negro Race in America from 1619 to 1880.* Five years later, he published his *History of Negro Troops in the War of Rebellion, 1861–1865,* making him the first major African American historian.

In a brief eight years after his first book was published, Williams visited the Congo in Africa, wrote a landmark article against colonialism, and served as a U.S. diplomat in Haiti from 1885–1886. Later, he moved to England, where he did research. Sadly, he died from a mysterious illness in 1891.

PART THREE

◆

INTO THE NEW CENTURY

LIEUTENANT HENRY O.
FLIPPER

(1856–1940)

Henry Ossian Flipper was the first African American to graduate from West Point, the United States Military Academy.

Flipper was born in slavery in Thomasville, Georgia, on March 31, 1856. His mother, Isabella Buckhalter, was the slave of the Reverend Reuben H. Lucky. His father, Festus Flipper, a skilled shoemaker, belonged to Ephraim G. Ponder. Isabella and Festus had to get permission from their masters to marry and start a family. Henry was the firstborn of their five boys.

When the Civil War broke out, Ephraim Ponder, like many other Southern slave owners, decided to move his people to a safer place. He chose Atlanta. Festus Flipper arranged to purchase his wife and sons so they could all move to Atlanta with Ponder.

When the Civil War ended, the Flipper family, all free now, remained in Atlanta. Festus Flipper set up shop as a shoemaker. Henry and his brothers attended schools run by the American Missionary Association. A Ponder slave had taught Henry how to read. He was an eager student, who grew up to attend Atlanta University.

Recognizing Flipper's ability, James Crawford Freeman of Griffin, Georgia, a black man elected to the U.S. House of Representatives during Reconstruction, appointed him to West Point.

Two other young black men had been appointed to West Point in 1870. Michael Howard had failed his courses and had to leave. James Webster Smith, of South Carolina, had more luck, but he had difficulty keeping up with his academic work and had to repeat a year.

Flipper arrived at West Point in 1873 and was assigned a room with James Webster Smith. But Smith, despite protests, was eventually discharged from the academy.

Left alone, Flipper faced the daunting life of a black cadet at West Point. He did not complain. In fact, he stated that he was generally treated as a peer. He concentrated on his studies, learning Spanish and majoring in civil engineering. He too had "academic deficiencies" and graduated fiftieth in a class of seventy-six in June 1877. Nevertheless, as the first black graduate of West Point, he was hailed for his achievement by blacks in the cities of the North. It was a milestone.

In November 1880, Lieutenant Flipper was posted to Fort Davis in the Oklahoma Territory. At Fort Davis, Flipper oversaw the everyday, nonmilitary supplies that the men could purchase at the post exchange, the fort's general store.

The commanding officer of Fort Davis at the time was Colonel W. R. Shafter, who had commanded several all-black units in the Civil War, notably the Seventeenth United States Colored Infantry. Less than a year after Flipper's posting to Fort Davis, Colonel Shafter claimed Flipper had embezzled $3,971.77. He said Flipper had failed to mail this amount of money to the proper officer and that he, Shafter, had seen Flipper in town, on horseback, with saddlebags. Supposedly fearing that Flipper was about to leave town, Shafter had him arrested.

At the court-martial that followed, Flipper faced two charges. He offered an explanation of the deficit that was convincing enough to

THE BUFFALO SOLDIER

Second Lieutenant Henry O. Flipper was the first black assigned to a command position in a black unit after the Civil War. In July 1866, while Flipper was at West Point, Congress had authorized the first peacetime units of African American soldiers. Legislation established two cavalry and four infantry regiments (later consolidated into two) of African Americans. The majority had served in all-black units during the Civil War. Mounted on horses, the Ninth and Tenth Cavalries rode on the frontier. The Cheyenne and Comanche Indians nicknamed them Buffalo Soldiers.

♦ The **cavalry** travels long distances on horseback or in vehicles during their combat missions.

♦ An **infantry** is made up of soldiers trained, armed, and equipped to fight on foot.

The cavalrymen of the Ninth and Tenth protected settlers from the Indians. They also explored and mapped vast areas of the Southwest, strung hundreds of miles of telegraph lines, and built and repaired frontier outposts. They also protected the crews of the ever-expanding railroads from Indians and outlaws. The Buffalo Soldiers consistently received some of the worst assignments that the army had to offer. They faced severe prejudice from the citizens of the postwar frontier towns. Nevertheless, they developed into two of the most distinguished fighting units in the army.

Flipper joined the Tenth Calvary in Fort Sill in Oklahoma Territory. He later served at Fort Elliott and Fort Concho in Texas. He was involved in several fights with Apache, Comanche, and Kiowa Indians, on whose lands forts had been built.

cause the officers to find him not guilty on the charge of embezzlement. However, they did find him guilty of the second charge—conduct unbecoming an officer. This mysterious charge, never satisfactorily explained, was all the officers needed to dismiss him from service. The real story, according to some scholars, is that Flipper got into trouble by being a black officer who attempted to assert his social equality.

John M. Carroll, historian and author of the 1971 book *The Black Military Experience in the American West,* mentions a letter from a white officer at the post stating that the charges against Flipper had been trumped up. The charges were based not on any wrongdoing of Flipper's but on his daring to act as if he were a social equal to whites. That letter was subsequently destroyed in a fire, but even if it had been introduced at the court-martial, there is little likelihood that it would have swayed the judges.[1]

If Flipper hoped for justice by appealing to higher military authorities, he was disappointed. His dismissal was confirmed by President Chester A. Arthur and carried out on June 30, 1882.

Flipper remained in the Southwest. He put his studies of civil engineering and his knowledge of Spanish to good use, validating Spanish and Mexican land grants in the United States and translating the mining laws of Mexico into English. His translation of *Mexican Laws, Statutes,* into English was an important contribution to international law. The National Geographic Society, the Archeological

These Buffalo Soldiers, shown in Montana in 1894, served in the Tenth Cavalry. The Tenth spent twenty years in the Southwest during the Indian Wars.

Institute of America, and the Arizona Society of Civil Engineers invited him to become a member. Clearly, they considered him a gentleman and a professional.

When the Spanish-American War broke out in 1898, Flipper sought the restoration of his officer's commission in the army. Although Flipper had backing from several influential congressmen and newspapers, the army denied his request.

As the years passed, Flipper worked at several jobs: as an engineer for American mining companies in Mexico, as a translator for the Senate Committee on Foreign Relations, and as an assistant to the Secretary of the Interior.

In his retirement, Flipper lived with his brother, Bishop Joseph Flipper, in Atlanta. Bishop Flipper was an ordained minister in the African Methodist Episcopal Church. The other Flipper sons had done well, too. Festus Jr. was a wealthy farmer in Thomasville; Carl was a professor in Savannah, Georgia; and E. H. earned his medical degree and became a physician in Jacksonville, Florida. But only Henry O. Flipper would go into the record books as a man who had cared deeply about the army and wanted to serve it, but was denied the right to serve even after repeated attempts to vindicate himself. He had to be content with publishing his version of the events in *Negro Frontiersman: The Western Memoirs of Henry O. Flipper.*

After Flipper died on May 3, 1940, at the age of eighty-four, his brother Joseph completed the death certificate. For "occupation," he wrote "Retired Army Officer." Years later, the court-martial sentence was reversed. Lieutenant Flipper's remains were reburied with full honors in Arlington National Cemetery.

COLONEL CHARLES A.
YOUNG

(1864–1922)

The third African American to graduate from West Point, Charles A. Young was born on March 12, 1864, in Macon County, Kentucky, the son of a former slave. At the age of nine, he moved with his family to Ripley, Ohio, where he attended local schools and graduated from Ripley's Colored High School in 1880. In 1884, he was appointed to the United States Military Academy at West Point, becoming the ninth African American cadet in its history. When he graduated in 1889, he was the last black to do so for half a century.

After his graduation, Young was commissioned as a second lieutenant and assigned to the Ninth Cavalry Regiment at Fort Robinson, Nebraska. Like other Buffalo Soldiers, Young suffered extreme prejudice from white officers who resented commanding blacks. Army records include complaints of his "tactical errors" as officer of the guard, neglect of "stable duty," and other reprimands. Nevertheless, Young realized that he was lucky compared to most blacks, and he stuck with it. Transferred to Fort Duchesne, Utah, in 1891, he was

✦ INTO THE NEW CENTURY ✦

named officer-in-charge and teacher of the post school, where he served until 1894.

On the death in 1894 of John Hanks Alexander, the second African American to graduate from West Point, Young succeeded Alexander as a professor of military science at Wilberforce University, a black college in Ohio. At Wilberforce, he taught tactics, military science, mathematics, and French. Two years later, he was directed to appear before the examining board at Fort Leavenworth, Kansas, for possible promotion to first lieutenant. Young traveled to Fort Leavenworth but was unable to find a place to stay in the town. He had to stay in Kansas City and travel to the fort for his examination. He passed the exam and was promoted to first lieutenant, with a salary of $1,800 a year.

♦ To be **commissioned** is to be granted the military rank and authority of an officer.

♦ **Tactics** is the skill of planning and directing the movements of military forces in combat.

♦ A **battalion** is a military unit made up of a headquarters and two or more companies.

♦ A **military attaché** is a military expert who serves his or her country as a diplomat in a foreign land.

Two years later, in May 1898, Young was called to serve in the Spanish-American War. Assigned to command the Ninth Ohio Volunteer Infantry, an African American unit, he was said to be the first colored officer to command a battalion in the army. Young's unit saw no action in that brief war, which was over by August 1898.

In February 1901, Young was promoted to captain and sent to the Philippines, where he commanded troops in the jungle facing Philippine guerrilla fighters.

In 1902, Young was named acting superintendent of two national parks in California, Sequoia and General Grant (the army patrolled the parks until the creation of the National Parks Service in 1916). He traveled to San Francisco from Manila, Philippines, on the ship *Sheridan*. According to an article in the December 27, 1902, issue of the Indianapolis *Freeman*, a black newspaper, Young was very popular among the

Medics carry a wounded officer from a battleground during the brief Spanish-American War.

passengers: "His skin is of the darkest hue of the race, but he is exceedingly clever, a West Point graduate, and a pianist of rare ability."[1]

Headquartered at the Presidio, U.S. Army headquarters in San Francisco, Young got along well with others. The Indianapolis *Freeman* reported that he was among the army officers feted at a banquet given by Lieutenant B. R. Tillman of South Carolina, whose father was a notorious segregationist. Asked if he had not made a mistake in including Young, Lieutenant Tillman responded, "No, he is a gentleman and a friend of mine."[2]

While in San Francisco, Young was promoted to colonel and in 1904 became the first African American military attaché, assigned to Haiti and Santo Domingo. He spent three years there, making maps of the two contiguous countries and reporting on their society and government.

Young returned to the United States in 1907 and spent a year at Wilberforce University, where he raised funds for a monument to the

African American poet Paul Laurence Dunbar. He managed to collect about $500, mostly from whites. But that was not Young's top priority. He was rising rapidly in the ranks. By 1909, Young had served in the Philippines, had been promoted to captain, and commanded the third squadron of the Ninth Cavalry in Wyoming.

At the urging of Booker T. Washington, founder of the all-black Tuskegee Institute in Alabama and the most influential African American in the United States, Young then accepted the post of military attaché to Liberia, the African nation founded by free blacks in the nineteenth century. He personally chose the three men who accompanied him, and the four drew maps of the country, reorganized the Liberian Frontier Force and police, and assisted the Liberian government in settling its many border disputes. One of his group, Wilson Ballard, became a major in the Liberian Defense Forces. Young saw military action in Liberia, leading a successful effort to suppress the

COLONEL YOUNG TO THE RESCUE

Young was dispatched to Mexico to lead the Tenth Cavalry Regiment in expeditions against Francisco "Pancho" Villa, a leader in the Mexican Revolution of 1910–1911. Villa was held responsible for the 1916 raid against the U.S. town of Columbus, New Mexico. Although U.S. forces pursued Villa throughout the Mexican state of Chihuahua, they not only failed to capture him but became trapped by his men. Nevertheless, Charles Young was commended by his commanding officers for leading successful charges at Aguascalientes and Santa Cruz de Villegas, Chihuahua, to rescue the all-white Thirteenth Cavalry from Villa's forces.

Major Frank Tompkins of the Thirteenth said, "By God, Young, I could kiss every black face out there." Young, unsmiling, responded, "Well, Tompkins, if you want to, you may start with me."[3] Young was promoted to lieutenant colonel.

revolt of the coastal Croo people and suffering a slight wound in a similar action. Promoted to major in the fall of 1911, he achieved the highest rank of any black officer in the army, except for chaplains.

In 1915, despite the protests of the Liberian government and the U.S. State Department, the army recalled Young, who in 1916 was awarded the Spingarn Medal, the highest honor bestowed by the National Association for the Advancement of Colored People (NAACP) "for the Afro-American male or female who has made the highest achievement during the preceding year in any field of elevated or honorable human endeavor."

In 1917, Young established a school for black soldiers at Fort Huachuca, Arizona. World War I broke out soon afterward, and Congress created a black division of the army. Young, the highest-ranking officer in the service, expected to lead it. But in June 1917, when he underwent a medical examination for promotion to full colonel, he was deemed physically unfit. After further tests at San Francisco's Letterman General Hospital, doctors certified that he suffered from high blood pressure and that his condition was life-threatening.

Young had suffered from high blood pressure for several years. He also had nephritis, a chronic inflammation of the kidneys. But neither condition had prevented him from doing his duty. Certain that the army's command was using his condition as an excuse to deny him the promotion he wanted, Young protested that he had never missed a day's service other than during his recuperation from a minor wound in Liberia. To prove his fitness, he rode on horseback from Ohio to Washington, D.C. Influential people, both white and black, including W. E. B. Du Bois, the well-known black intellectual regarded as the founder of black nationalism, rallied to Young's defense, but to no avail. He was retired from active duty and promoted to colonel on the inactive list. Not until November 1918, just five days before the armistice officially ending World War I was signed, was he reinstated to active duty.

Young spent several months with the Ohio National Guard before being recalled to Liberia as a government adviser in 1919. While there, his health began to fail; but he continued to serve and was in Lagos, Nigeria, in early 1922 when he died of nephritis. His body was returned to the United States where he was buried with full military honors in Arlington National Cemetery. Seven years later, in May 1929, Camp No. 24, National Indian War Veterans, in Washington, D.C., became the first all-black army camp. Its members chose to honor Charles Young by naming their camp after him. Colonel Young's house in Wilberforce, Ohio, has been declared a national landmark.

BRIGADIER GENERAL BENJAMIN O. DAVIS SR.

(1877–1970)

Benjamin O. Davis entered the world just as Reconstruction was ending. He was born on July 1, 1877, into a comfortable family in Washington, D.C. His mother was Henrietta Stewart Davis. His father, Louis Patrick Henry Davis, had spent his boyhood as a servant in the home of General and Mrs. John A. Logan. General Logan eventually became a U.S. representative and a U.S. senator for Illinois. Louis Davis had accompanied the general to Washington, D.C., where Logan helped him get a job with the Department of the Interior. Louis Davis purchased a home at 1830 11th Street, N.W., and became part of the district's middle class.

Benjamin O. Davis attended Washington's all-black M Street High School, where he received his first military training as a cadet. He liked the discipline and order. When he enrolled at Howard University, he joined the Eighth U.S. Volunteer Infantry, the black unit of the District of Columbia National Guard. He was commissioned a first lieutenant and decided that he wanted a military career. When he confided his desire to his father, the older man advised against

enlisting. A man who had grown up with a general, Louis Davis determined that his son would attend the United States Military Academy at West Point, New York, and become a commissioned officer.

Since they had no representatives in Congress, residents of the District of Columbia could be appointed to the academy only by the president of the United States. Louis Davis asked General Logan to use his influence with President William McKinley. But for political reasons, President McKinley would not appoint a black man to the academy. Black equal rights had few defenders at the turn of the century, and McKinley had no desire to stir up the issue. Benjamin O. Davis had no choice. He decided to enlist in the army and work his way up to a commission. This decision caused an estrangement from his father that lasted almost until the older man's death in 1921.

Davis took his oath as a private on June 14, 1899, and joined Troop I, Ninth Cavalry, stationed at Fort Duchesne, Utah. He soon learned that what his father had said was true. His pay as a private was just $25 a month, and Davis was the only man in his troop who could read and write. His knowledge and his willingness to work caught the attention of his superiors. In 1901, commissioned a second lieutenant, he joined Charles Young, who had graduated from West Point in 1899, as the only other black regular line officer in the army.

Second Lieutenant Davis belonged to a cavalry unit assigned to the Philippines during an uprising there. While on leave in October 1902, he married Elnora Dickerson, a neighbor and former schoolmate. They eventually had three children—Olive, Benjamin Jr., and Nora.

Army life entails moving around a great deal. Benjamin Davis and his family moved more than most. Why? His superiors did not want Davis to command white troops or mix with white officers. He had occasional battlefront assignments, such as on the Mexican border in 1912 during the Mexican Revolution. But he mainly received "safe" postings, such as commanding Reserve Officer Training Corps (ROTC) units at black colleges or black National Guard units and serving as

THE FIRST BRIGADIER GENERAL

In 1940, Benjamin O. Davis was promoted to brigadier general, the first African American general since the Reconstruction period—and the first African American general in the regular army. Black generals during Reconstruction held their positions in the state militia or National Guard units. General Davis had been the commanding officer of the 369th Infantry, New York National Guard, before his promotion. The 369th would later distinguish itself in World War II as the Harlem Hellfighters.

During World War II, General Davis served as a special adviser and coordinator in the European theater of operations. In 1945, he was appointed an assistant to the inspector general and later a special assistant to the Secretary of the Army. In that capacity, he worked hard for equal rights for black soldiers and for their integration into the regular army. In 1948, President Harry S. Truman issued an executive order to that effect. General Davis retired a few months later.

military attaché to the American Legation, Monrovia, Liberia, in 1911–1912. While continually writing letters to the War Department requesting duty with troops, Davis did the jobs he was assigned. In 1915, he was promoted to captain and, shortly after, to major and lieutenant colonel.

In 1916, Davis was teaching at all-black Wilberforce University in Ohio. That year, nine days after the birth of their third child, Davis's wife, Elnora, died. Shortly thereafter, assigned to duty in the Philippines, Davis took the children to Washington, D.C., to be cared for by his parents. While in the Philippines, he courted a family friend, Sadie Overton, by mail. They were married in 1919. Davis returned to the United States to take up duties as a professor of military science and tactics at all-black Tuskegee Institute in Alabama. His family was now reunited.

World War I had come and gone, and Davis had not been assigned a real combat position. He was also still among the only black officers in the army, including the chaplains in the Ninth and Tenth Cavalry regiments and the Twenty-fourth and Twenty-fifth Infantry regiments. Promoted to full colonel in 1930, Davis remained at that rank for ten years. It took the pressures of World War II to force his promotion to brigadier general.

Although Benjamin O. Davis Sr. had been awarded a variety of medals during his career—including the Distinguished Service Cross, the Bronze Star, and the French Croix de Guerre with Palm, he never had the opportunity to win medals in combat. He did, however, live to see his son, Benjamin O. Davis Jr., achieve what his own times had denied him. After his son, Colonel Davis Jr., won the Distinguished Flying Cross as commander of the Ninety-ninth Fighter Squadron, 332d Fighter Group, in the Italian theater, General Davis Sr. flew to Italy to personally pin the medal on his son's uniform. General Davis died in 1970.

PRIVATE HENRY
JOHNSON

(1897–1929)

Only about 50,000 black soldiers actually saw combat with the U.S. armed forces during World War I. Henry Johnson, born in Albany, New York, was among them. He is perhaps the most famous African American soldier who served in World War I. During that war, some 400,000 blacks entered into military service. But very few got combat assignments. Instead, the vast majority were charged with loading and unloading ships, salvaging war materials, building fortifications, detonating explosives, and burying the dead. The first black battalion was sent to France not long after the United States declared war on Germany and the other Central powers. By the time the war was over, black soldier-workers were a third of the U.S. forces on the European continent.

Johnson was a redcap, or railroad porter, when the war broke out. He enlisted in the Fifteenth National Guard of New York, which during the war became the 369th Infantry—the first unit of black combat troops to arrive in Europe. They landed in December 1917 to support

French troops at Bois d'Hauza. That spring, the African Americans withstood German attacks for about two months.

On the night of May 15, 1918, Henry Johnson and fellow private Needham Roberts were doing guard duty at an outpost not far from enemy lines, and they personally prevented a German sneak attack.

According to Henry Johnson's account, his superior officer had wanted to send out two newly drafted men for the midnight-to-four watch. Johnson protested. "I told him he was crazy to send untrained men out there and risk the rest of us," said Johnson. "I said I'd tackle the

THEY CAME FROM ALL SIDES

Henry Johnson never forgot the night that he and Needham Roberts faced the enemy alone. "Somewhere around two o'clock I heard the Germans cutting our wire out in front and I called to Roberts. When he came, I told him to pass the word to the lieutenant. He had just started off when the snippin' and clippin' of the wires sounded near, so I let go with a hand grenade. There was a yell from a lot of surprised [Germans] and then they started firing. I hollered to Needham to come back. A German grenade got Needham in the arm and through the hip.

✦ A **trench** is a long, narrow depression in the ground used for military defense.

He was too badly wounded to do any fighting, so I told him to lie in the trench and hand me up the grenades. Keep your nerve, I told him."[1]

Johnson kept throwing grenades at the Germans. They came from all sides. When the grenades ran out, Johnson started shooting with his rifle. But when he tried to load a U.S. cartridge clip into the French rifle, the clip jammed. Johnson then used the rifle as a club until it broke. Grabbing his French bolo knife, he began to slash wildly about until he saw that some Germans had seized Roberts and were dragging him off. Johnson leapt on one of the men's shoulders and stabbed him. He stuck another in the stomach and flailed about with his knife in all directions. The rest of the Germans fled, leaving Needham Roberts behind. Henry Johnson lived to tell the story.

As crowds cheer, the 369th, one of the most decorated fighting units of World War I, takes a victory march up New York City's Fifth Avenue.

job, though I needed sleep. German snipers had been shooting our way that night, and I told the corporal he wanted men on the job who knew their rifles. He said it was my imagination, but anyway he took those green men off and left Needham and me on the posts."[2]

When that night's battle was over, four German soldiers lay dead, and seven pairs of wire cutters, three German Lugers, and forty hand grenades had been abandoned.

The "Battle of Henry Johnson" made headlines in U.S. and Allied newspapers. Meanwhile, its hero spent weeks in French hospitals. Most of the bones had to be removed from his shattered foot; a shinbone was replaced with a silver tube; and a half-dozen permanent scars marked the rest of his body. During Johnson's time in the hospital, he was promoted to sergeant. He and Roberts became the first U.S. soldiers in the war to receive individually the Croix de Guerre, France's highest honor for bravery in action.

On November 17, 1918, French troops and their U.S. support troops marched onto German soil. The French government gave the 369th Infantry regiment the honor of being the first Allied unit to enter Germany. The 369th had not lost a single man, had never retreated, and had already been cited for bravery eleven times. The French government awarded the entire regiment the high honor of its Croix de Guerre.

Private Henry Johnson died in 1929. In 1987, a bronze bust in his honor was unveiled in his hometown of Albany, New York.

◆

PART FOUR

MODERN TIMES

MAJOR GENERAL BENJAMIN O. DAVIS JR.

(B. 1912)

The career of Benjamin O. Davis Jr. almost tells the story of African Americans in the military in the twentieth century. Like his father before him, he was a pioneer in the military; but he would have even more success because of the changing times.

Davis was born on December 18, 1912, at just about the time his father, Benjamin O. Davis Sr., was assigned to service in the Mexican Border Patrol. Benjamin Jr. was only four years old when his mother, Elnora Dickerson Davis, died after giving birth to her third child. For a time, his father took care of the children with help from Elnora's sisters. But when Davis Sr. was posted to the Philippines, he sent the children to live with his parents in Washington, D.C. Three years later, Davis Sr. remarried, and the children went to live with him and their stepmother in Tuskegee, Alabama, where he taught military science and tactics at all-black Tuskegee Institute.

Benjamin Jr. was a typical "army brat." He moved often and learned early to adjust to new surroundings. He started public school

at Tuskegee and finished in Cleveland, Ohio, at Central High School. In his senior year he was elected president of the student council.

Davis then enrolled at Western Reserve University but transferred to the University of Chicago, where he majored in mathematics. He made the move to Chicago because his father wanted him to go to the U.S. Military Academy at West Point. Chicago had a black congressman, Oscar De Priest, who would be able to appoint Davis to the academy. Davis was not so sure he wanted to follow in his father's footsteps, however. He had heard about the extreme prejudice at the academy. No black had graduated since Charles Young nearly fifty years before. And Davis knew firsthand about the segregation in the army, where his father had served in all-black units for his entire career. He did not approach the West Point entrance examination with enthusiasm. Still, it was a jolt when he learned that he had failed the test.

That failure was the spur that Davis needed. He determined he would prove—to his father and to himself—that he could not only qualify for the academy but do well. Reappointed by De Priest, he studied hard for the examination and passed. He entered West Point on July 1, 1923.

Resentful of someone different in their midst, the other cadets subjected Davis to the "silent treatment." For an entire year, no one spoke to him unless absolutely necessary. At the end of that plebe year, he was congratulated by some of his classmates, but the silence soon descended again. For his entire four years at West Point, he never had a roommate. But he did not complain—not even to his father. He realized that complaining would only make things worse, and that there was little he could do but stick it out and try to maintain his dignity as best he could.

+ A **plebe** is a first-year cadet at a U.S. military academy.

+ A **squadron** is a unit of the U.S. Air Force.

+ **Strafing** is a low-flying aircraft's machine-gun fire onto ground troops.

The Winds of World War II

In September 1939 Nazi forces under German leader Adolf Hitler invaded Poland and moved west, taking France in June 1940. England suffered under massive German bombing raids from August through October 1940. Many people in the United States were against entering the war to help England, but President Franklin D. Roosevelt believed that the country should be prepared for war. Not only was the Nazi threat real, but U.S. relations with Germany's ally Japan were deteriorating. It was time for action.

The Army Air Corps (there was no separate air force at the time) rushed to train more pilots. Pressured by black civil rights groups such as the NAACP, the Army Air Corps established an Advanced Army Flying School at Tuskegee Institute. Benjamin O. Davis Jr. was in the first class of thirteen aviation cadets at Tuskegee.

At his graduation on June 12, 1936, Davis received his diploma from General John J. Pershing and his commission as a second lieutenant. He also received a rash of publicity as the first black West Point graduate in the twentieth century. That same year, he married Agatha Scott of New Haven, Connecticut, whom he had met in his junior year at the academy. The newlyweds traveled to Davis's first posting—Fort Benning, Georgia, in the heart of the segregated South.

Davis was promoted to first lieutenant in 1937, and two years later to captain. Every year, he was posted somewhere else. He worried that like his father he would be shuttled around as the army tried to find something for him to do that would not involve commanding white troops. But by the time he was promoted to captain, World War II would change everything.

On December 7, 1941, while Davis was at Tuskegee learning to fly, Japan bombed the U.S. Pacific Fleet at Pearl Harbor, Hawaii. After Pearl Harbor, there was no escape from the conflict that consumed the rest of the world. The United States entered World War II.

Davis was eager to get into the action, but the U.S. Army was not yet ready for a black flying squadron. Following graduation in the spring of 1942, Davis was appointed commandant of cadets at Tuskegee. He concentrated on excellence. He planned to be ready when the new U.S. Air Force allowed black fliers into the fight.

Finally, in early April 1943, the Ninety-ninth Pursuit Squadron, made up of airmen trained at Tuskegee and under the command of Colonel Benjamin O. Davis Jr., headed to North Africa, where Germany and its ally Italy were trying to gain control. On June 2, flying a strafing mission over an island off Sicily, the Ninety-ninth saw its first combat—but not the last. Early in July, the Ninety-ninth invaded Sicily and helped to capture it. Afterward, Davis took charge of the 332d Fighter Group, which included three new squadrons and several support units. He returned to the United States, where a different kind of fight awaited him: attempts were being made to prevent black flying units from being assigned to combat areas. Davis testified forcefully to the competence and courage of his men. His persistence paid off.

Benjamin O. Davis Jr.'s 332d Fighter Group, the Tuskegee Airmen, listen for their orders.

Colonel Benjamin O. Davis Jr. stands at attention with his fellow officers as his father, Brigadier General Benjamin O. Davis Sr., pins the Distinguished Flying Cross on his uniform.

In 1944, Davis's 332d finally headed out again for the Italian front. Soon joined by the 99th Pursuit Squadron, the 332d was the largest fighter group there. They soon gained a reputation as skilled bomber escorts. It was deadly work. In October, a total of fifteen African American pilots were downed during their missions. The following April, after winter weather halted the air war, they flew fifty-four combat missions. They lost several planes and pilots but also shot down seventeen enemy aircraft.

In April 1945, Germany surrendered; and in August, Japan surrendered. The war was over. General Benjamin O. Davis Sr. flew to Italy to personally pin the Distinguished Flying Cross on the uniform of his son, Colonel Benjamin O. Davis Jr.

Davis's next assignment was to head the 447th Bombardment Group, a newly trained black flying unit formed in 1943 under pressure from black groups and some members of Congress. The air force had no real intention of sending relatively inexperienced pilots on bombing missions and had hoped that the war would end before the

447th was sent into action. The war did end, and a new era was about to begin. President Roosevelt died in 1945, and his vice president, Harry S. Truman, assumed the presidency. In 1948, President Truman established a commission on equal treatment and opportunity for blacks in the armed services. Both General Davis and Colonel Davis testified before that commission that segregation was harmful not only to black servicemen but also to the armed services in general. The new Secretary of the Air Force, Stuart Symington, decided that Colonel Davis's 332d would be the first all-black unit to be integrated into the larger air force.

Davis continued to receive promotions. Over the next two decades, he was named brigadier general (while serving in the Korean War in 1955) and later Chief of Staff, United Nations Command, the second highest position in the United Nations military. He became the first black to command an air base, Godman Field in Kentucky. He retired in 1970 at the age of fifty-seven, with the rank of permanent major general. In addition to the Distinguished Flying Cross, his medals included the Air Medal with four Oak Leaf Clusters, the Legion of Merit Award, and the French Croix de Guerre with Palm.

During General Davis's long career, blacks had managed to integrate just about all levels of the service, but Davis was "the only" or "the first" black in his positions and commands. In 1971, one year after his retirement, black officers still represented less than 2 percent of all the air force officers. But General Benjamin O. Davis Jr. was proud of his country's achievement. He entitled his autobiography *Benjamin O. Davis, Jr., American.*

LIEUTENANT COLONEL
CHARITY ADAMS
EARLEY

(B. 1918)

The commanding officer of the only organization of black women to serve overseas during World War II was Charity Edna Adams. She was born on December 5, 1918, in Kittrell, North Carolina, the oldest child of the Reverend Eugene Adams and Charity A. Adams. She attended segregated schools, graduated from high school as valedictorian of her class, and earned a scholarship to Wilberforce University in Wilberforce, Ohio. Graduating from Wilberforce with a bachelor's degree in 1938, she taught mathematics and science in the segregated schools of Columbia, South Carolina, for the years 1938–1942.

The dean of women at Wilberforce University recommended Adams for the Women's Army Auxiliary Corps (WAAC), and Adams applied. Sworn in on July 13, 1942, she was stationed at Fort Des Moines in Iowa, one of forty black women who entered the first WAAC officer candidate class; she was commissioned on August 29, 1942.

If Charity Adams expected to go overseas, she was disappointed. There were plans to send the black women to war, but Oveta Culp Hobby, director of the Women's Army Corps, refused to let them go.

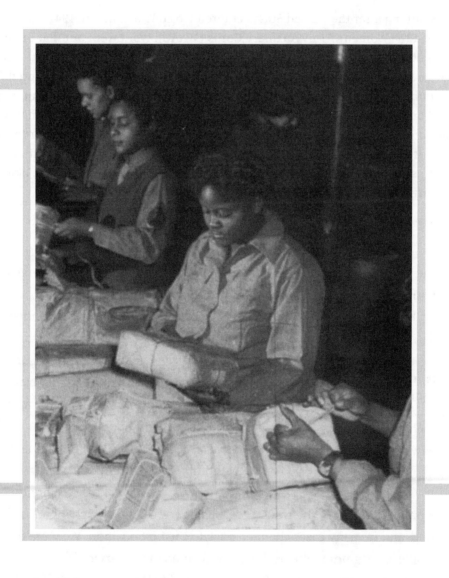

THE WOMEN'S ARMY

Not long after the United States entered World War II in late 1941, the army formed the Women's Army Auxiliary Corps (WAAC). Word went out that up to 10 percent of the force would be black. This was big news, since at the time, the navy did not accept black women into its women's corps, the Women Accepted for Voluntary Emergency Service (WAVE). The WAAC served with the army but, as an auxiliary force, was not part of it. On July 3, 1943, Congress passed a bill that converted WAAC into the Women's Army Corps (WAC), which would be part of the army itself. All members, known as Wacs, were given the choice of joining the army as a member of the WAC or returning to civilian life. Charity Adams, like the majority, joined the new women's army.

The plans were quickly canceled. That was just one of many changes women like Charity Adams went through.

For six weeks, both black and white officer candidates attended classes and ate together. But their platoons, post clubs, theaters, and beauty shops were segregated. Adams took it in stride. As she recalled, her class "was the guinea pig for the WAAC, and lots of adjustments had to be made on both sides, by the trainees and the trainers. We were subjected to hundreds of changes during that first six weeks. We were the people upon whom the rules and policies were tried out, changed and tried, and in many cases changed back to the first position. We were the people . . . beginning the tradition for women in the service."[1]

+ A **platoon** is made up of two or more **squads** of troops; a squad is the smallest unit of military personnel.

+ A **convoy** is an accompanying or protecting force.

Pressure from the NAACP and the National Urban League finally forced the War Department to direct the European theater to accept black Wacs.

In early January 1945, some 500 black Wacs were assembled at the Extended Field Service Battalion, Third WAC Training Center, Fort Oglethorpe, Georgia, where they received overseas training and were outfitted for overseas duty. This preparation included doing a 5-mile hike in full regalia (pistol belts, gas masks, canteens, packs, and helmets) under active war conditions and learning how to climb up and down a cargo net and go through a gas chamber. At the end of January, the 500 women boarded a train and went to Camp Shanks, New York, for final processing for overseas. A ferry transported them to the *Ile-de-France,* and accompanied by an armed convoy of ships, they arrived in Scotland on February 12 and boarded a train for Birmingham, England. There, Charity Adams assumed command of the 6888th Central Postal Directory Battalion. Brigadier General Benjamin O. Davis, the highest-ranking black male commissioned officer, greeted them on their arrival.

From Birmingham, England, to Rouen, France, to Paris, France, Charity Adams led the 6888th. In each place, they made sure the mail got to all U.S. personnel in the European theater of operations (including army, navy, Marine Corps, civilians, and Red Cross workers), a total of over 7 million people. The 6888th kept an updated information card on each person in the theater. Some personnel on the front moved frequently, often requiring several information updates per month. The Wacs worked three eight-hour shifts, seven days a week, to clear out the tremendous backlog of Christmas mail. The 6888th broke all records for redirecting mail to and from the troops over which it had authority. While overseeing the mail, Adams fought her own battles against segregated living quarters and recreational facilities and the general under whose command her battalion operated.

One day, the general reviewing Adams's troops found fault. She protested, and the general said that he would find a white junior officer to show her how to do her job. When she replied "Over my dead body, sir," he threatened a court-martial. But when Major Adams and her staff started to file court-martial charges against the general for violating a policy that forbade "racial emphasis" in any verbal or written commands or reports, the general dropped his charges.

Germany surrendered on May 8, 1945, and in December the 6888th was disbanded. Charity Adams was discharged in 1946 with the rank of lieutenant colonel, the highest rank below that of the WAC director.

Lieutenant Colonel Adams chose not to remain in the military. Like thousands of other veterans, she used the GI Bill to continue her education, earning her M.A. in vocational psychology from Ohio State University. She worked as a registration officer for the Veterans Administration in Cleveland, Ohio; as an assistant professor of education at Georgia State College (now Savannah State University) in Savannah, Georgia; and as an employment and personnel counselor for the YWCA in New York City.

In 1949, Adams married Stanley A. Earley Jr., a medical student at the University of Zurich, and moved with him to Switzerland. She then undertook further study in psychology at the University of Zurich and at the Jungian Institute of Analytical Psychology. After the Earleys' return to the United States and the birth of their two children, they settled in Dayton, Ohio.

In 1982, Earley was honored by the Smithsonian Institution in a salute to 110 of the most important women in black history. That same year, she accepted the NAACP's Walter White Award for her pioneering service. In 1989, Earley published *One Woman's Army: A Black Officer Remembers the WAC*, about her experiences and those of other first women in the army.

In 1991, Earley was awarded honorary doctorates in humane letters by both Wilberforce University and the University of Dayton. On her retirement from the board of directors of Dayton Power and Light, a scholarship at Wilberforce University was established in her honor.

Seaman Dorie
MILLER

(1919–1943)

Born October 12, 1919, on a farm near Waco, Texas, not long after World War I ended, Doris Miller preferred to be called Dorie. The son of sharecroppers, Dorie was a large boy and grew to be a strapping 200-pound star fullback on the Moore High School football team in Waco. After graduation, he went to work on his father's farm.

Miller was nineteen years old when he enlisted in the navy. At the time, the United States Navy offered few opportunities for black men. They could not expect to rise in the ranks or even to serve in combat positions. But for Dorie, the navy still offered more opportunities than he could expect from the life he knew in Waco. Besides, he wanted to travel.

After training at the Naval Training Station in Norfolk, Virginia, Mess Attendant Second Class Miller boarded the USS *West Virginia.* He would not be disappointed with his decision to leave home. Although his job was waiting tables in the mess hall, Miller enjoyed being on the ship, and he liked traveling to exotic ports. In December 1941, the *West Virginia* docked at the naval base at Pearl Harbor,

"above and beyond the call of duty"

DORIE MILLER
Received the Navy Cross
at Pearl Harbor, May 27, 1942

Hawaii. Miller looked forward to being there. His first three-year enlistment was nearly up; he intended to re-enlist.

Early in the morning of December 7, 1941, Miller was on breakfast duty below decks. He heard a distant explosion, but he thought little of it, being accustomed to hearing such sounds. He did not know then that Japan had decided to attack the U.S. Pacific Fleet at a time when the entire fleet was anchored at Pearl Harbor. The first Japanese bomb hit the seaplane hangers at the tip of Ford Island. Then a torpedo slammed into the battleship *Utah* across the island. Soon, all 400 Japanese attack planes had reached the area.

Dorie Miller, who had no training as a gunner, nevertheless performed that function. Amazingly, when the Japanese attack finally ended, Dorie Miller was unhurt. After a period of rest, he took up his

"AIR RAID!"

Aboard the *West Virginia*, on December 7, the public address system began to broadcast the alarm, "Air raid! Air raid! This is not a drill." Miller already knew they were under attack. Japanese planes rained bombs and torpedoes on the U.S. fleet. Explosion followed explosion. The sound was deafening.

Miller clambered up to the main deck just as a bomb tore into the ship's bridge, mortally wounding Captain Mervyn Bennion. Miller dragged his captain to a safer spot, where the man died. An ensign called to Miller to help pass ammunition to two machine gunners on the forward deck. Miller did as he was asked, all the while dodging bombs and torpedoes. Then one of the gunners he was helping was struck down. Half the guns were unmanned.

Leaping to the machine gun, Miller pointed it up to the sky. He had never before fired one of the anti-aircraft guns, yet he kept up a barrage of shots while a hail of enemy ammunition strafed the scarred deck.

Until all hands were ordered from the burning ship, Miller helped the Pearl Harbor fleet shoot down twenty-nine Japanese planes, personally accounting for four strikes until his ammunition ran out.

next assignment as a messman on the aircraft carrier USS *Liscome Bay*. He received a promotion to mess attendant third class, and Secretary of the Navy Frank Knox sent a personal note of commendation for his bravery.

While most reporters ignored Miller's heroism, the African American press covered it extensively. Black leaders pressured the Department of the Navy to honor Miller, and in the spring of 1942, in ceremonies aboard the USS *Liscome Bay*, Admiral Chester W. Nimitz, commander in chief of the Pacific Fleet, awarded Miller the Navy Cross, personally pinning the ribbon of this medallion to Miller's uniform and citing him for "distinguished devotion to duty, extraordinary courage and disregard for his own personal safety during the attack on Pearl Harbor."[1]

Miller himself was modest about his first experience in combat. "It wasn't hard. I just pulled the trigger and she worked fine. I had watched the others with these guns."[2]

In spite of this honor, Miller received no further promotions. Navy policy on black sailors remained intact, and Miller was assigned for training as a cook. In December 1943, Miller was among a crew of 700 men who were killed when a Japanese submarine torpedoed and sank the USS *Liscome Bay* in the South Pacific. A Dorie Miller Memorial Foundation was established in Chicago, and for many years after Miller's death, the foundation held a service in his honor. In New York City, a group of cooperative houses was named for him.

In 1971, a barracks at the Great Lakes training camp was named in his honor. In 1973, a destroyer-escort ship, the USS *Miller*, was commissioned in his memory; and in 1985, a memorial monument was erected at the Veterans Administration hospital in Waco, Texas. In 1988, a bill was introduced in the U.S. House of Representatives to award Seaman Miller a posthumous Congressional Medal of Honor. The bill failed to pass. It would have made him the first African American to receive the medal for bravery in World War II.

SECOND LIEUTENANT
VERNON J.
BAKER

(B. 1919)

Vernon J. Baker was born on December 17, 1919, in Cheyenne, Wyoming, the son of a carpenter. His parents died in an automobile crash when he was four years old. He and his two older sisters were raised by their grandparents. Cheyenne was a railroad hub, and Baker's grandfather worked as a head inspector for the Union Pacific Railroad, with the responsibility of checking each train's brakes. Railroad work was steady. Even during the Depression it put food on the table in his household.

Baker attended integrated schools in Cheyenne, and after graduating from high school, he followed his grandfather into railroad work. He got a job as a porter, but he subsequently lost that job. Unemployed, he attempted to enlist in the army in early 1941, as the United States geared up for war. When a recruiter put him off, telling him there were no quotas for blacks in the army, Baker was so insulted that he vowed not to return. But he continued to have trouble finding a job, and so he swallowed his pride and returned to the recruiting office. This time another recruiter accepted him.

Baker got a strong taste of racism when he boarded a bus to Texas for basic training. The bus driver called him nigger and ordered him to the back of the bus. At Camp Wolters in Mineral Wells, Texas, Baker was assigned to the area in the southwest corner of the camp reserved for Negro basic training and to the Twenty-fifth Infantry Regiment, the second oldest black unit in the army (after the Buffalo Soldiers of the Tenth Cavalry). On his first day, his sergeant asked if anyone could type. Baker raised his hand and was promptly named company clerk. One of his duties was to sign the payroll receipts of at least twenty-five of his fellow soldiers, who were illiterate and unable to sign their own names.

Baker was at the base movie theater when all soldiers were ordered to report to their barracks (lodgings). The Japanese navy had attacked the U.S. Pacific Fleet at Pearl Harbor, Hawaii, and the United States was now officially in World War II. A few days later, Baker was chosen for Officer Candidate School (OCS). There were thirty-one other blacks in his class—on the army fast track, since the service had very few black officers and was encountering resistance among white officers who did not want to command blacks.

Baker learned that he would be sent overseas when the white chief of staff of the Ninety-second Infantry Division announced to his OCS class, "All the white boys are going there getting killed. Now it's time for the colored boys to go get killed." [1]

Sent to Italy on the Mediterranean front to join the U.S. Fifth Army division, Baker, who held the rank of second lieutenant, distinguished himself early and was awarded a Bronze Star and a Purple Heart. He was wounded in October 1944 when a German bullet pierced his right forearm. Awakening in a military hospital after surgery, he angrily discovered that he was in a segregated ward.

In February 1945, units of the Fifth Army began an assault on Castle Aghinolfi, a German stronghold surrounded by three hills labeled X, Y, and Z. Baker's platoon was kept in reserve for two months; but at last, in early April, he and his comrades received orders to join the assault.

Word of Baker's heroics at Castle Aghinolfi spread throughout the division, and he was awarded both the Italian Cross of Valor and the

---

Behind Enemy Lines

Baker arose at 3:30 in the morning of April 5, 1945; ninety minutes later, he was leading his men toward Hill X. As they began to climb the hill, Baker ordered his men to step only on rocks. He knew that the Germans had placed mines all over the hill. As they advanced, the Americans stopped to clip the many yellow plastic-coated telephone lines that snaked along the ground and that enabled the Germans to track the U.S. soldiers' movements.

The platoon crossed the top of Hill X and skirted the edge of Hill Y. Baker spotted an enemy machine-gun nest and shot the Germans manning it. He then killed two Germans at another machine-gun position and disabled a rock-walled bunker.

At this point, his platoon was three miles behind enemy lines and headed for the castle. Baker continued on, disabling more hidden German fortifications. Suddenly, German rifle fire and grenades descended on the platoon, and Baker saw men dropping and being blown to pieces by mortars. The company commander, Captain John C. Runyon, decided to withdraw with the walking wounded and get reinforcements. Baker chose to remain.

Baker gathered together the living, who beat back three subsequent German attacks as they waited for reinforcements. When reinforcements did not come, he and the seven men remaining alive retreated. Only when he reached the bottom of Hill X and safety did Baker react to the carnage he had witnessed in the battle; he sat down at the side of the road and vomited.

The following morning, Baker returned to the battleground with the all-white 473d Battalion. But they found nothing except dead U.S. soldiers; the Germans had retreated. As he looked out over the mine craters and dead bodies, Baker suddenly became frightened over what might have happened to him.

Polish Cross of Valor. He and his commander, Captain Runyon, won the American Distinguished Service Cross. Baker's award made him the most highly decorated black U.S. soldier in

◆ A **bunker** is a protective underground chamber.

◆ A **mortar** is a weapon that fires missiles at high angles.

the Mediterranean theater. There was talk of his receiving the Congressional Medal of Honor, America's top award for bravery, but something happened to the paperwork. Captain Runyon, who was ordered to write a top-secret report of the battle, praised Baker's "magnificent courage." But the report was edited by top army officials. They downplayed Baker's heroism. The service hierarchy was far too racist to give a black man the nation's highest military honor. Indeed, no black soldier was awarded the Congressional Medal of Honor during World War II.

After the Germans surrendered, Baker remained in Italy as long as he could, enjoying the lack of racism he found there. He fell in love with an Italian woman and seriously considered taking her back to the United States. But reports of resentment against interracial relationships in his homeland caused him to reconsider. When the army posted him back home, he left his girlfriend in Italy.

Persuaded by an aunt to remain in the army, Baker joined the Eighty-second Airborne Division at the age of twenty-seven and became a paratrooper, a soldier trained and equipped to parachute from a plane. After the official order desegregating the military, he rose in the ranks and served in integrated companies around the world. While at Fort Huachuca, Arizona, where he'd started his army career after boot camp, Baker met and married Fern Brown, a native of Tucson. The couple had three daughters and adopted a Korean girl when the family was stationed in Southeast Asia. Baker was posted to Germany for his final tour of duty.

Baker left the army with the rank of second lieutenant at the age of forty-eight and went to work for the Red Cross, counseling military families. His wife died in 1986, and he retired from the Red Cross the following spring. He also moved to Benewah County in northern Idaho, a sparsely populated area where he had previously gone on hunting trips. In 1990, he married a German woman named Heidy Pawlik, joking that he had married the enemy, and settled down to a peaceful life among scattered neighbors who treated him as a human being and accepted his interracial marriage.

In 1989, after years of pressure from groups who knew that the role of blacks had been downplayed by a racist military hierarchy in World War II, Baker received a call from government researchers. They asked him about his service during the war, and he was suddenly forced to relive memories he had long buried. Finally, in January 1997, President Bill Clinton presented Baker with the Medal of Honor denied him fifty-one years earlier. Six other black veterans of the war were also awarded the honor. Seventy-seven years old, Second Lieutenant Baker was the only one still alive.

GENERAL DANIEL "CHAPPIE" JAMES JR.

(1920–1978)

Daniel "Chappie" James Jr. was born in Pensacola, Florida, on February 11, 1920, the youngest of seventeen children. Ten of the children died before Daniel was born. His father, Daniel James Sr., was a lamplighter until electricity arrived in Pensacola's black section; later, he worked in a gas plant. His mother, Lillie Anna Brown James, operated an elementary school for black children in her home. Chappie was one of his mother's students until the seventh grade, when he enrolled in Pensacola's Washington High School.

Growing up close to the United States Navy base in Pensacola, young James longed to be a navy pilot. Even though he understood that this career was closed to blacks, he held on to his dream. He enrolled at all-black Tuskegee Institute, where he majored in physical education and played tackle on the football team. Tuskegee proved to be the right place at the right time for James. The United States began to gear up for World War II, and Tuskegee became the first training center for black pilots. After graduating from Tuskegee with a bachelor of science degree, James enrolled in the Civilian Pilot

Program at Tuskegee and went from there to the Army Air Corps Aviation Cadet Program.

In the meantime, he married Dorothy Watkins, a fellow student at Tuskegee. The two would have a daughter and two sons.

Commissioned a second lieutenant, James took fighter pilot training at Selfridge Field in Michigan, but he never saw action in World War II. Instead, he trained pilots for the all-black Ninety-ninth Pursuit Squadron and piloted C-37 supply planes in the United States. He was a pilot, but he was not satisfied. At Freeman Field in Seymour, Indiana, on April 5, 1945, just before Germany surrendered and the war in Europe ended, Lieutenant James was among 100 black airmen who invaded the white officers club to protest segregation in the service. He was arrested, along with all the other protesters. Three were selected to stand trial. Thurgood Marshall, lead attorney for the NAACP, defended the men and won the case.

After the war and after President Harry S. Truman ordered that all the armed forces be racially integrated, James rose steadily in the ranks. Until 1949, he was assigned to Lockbourne Air Force Base in Ohio, after which he served in the Philippines as flight leader of the Twelfth Fighter Bomber Squadron based at Clark Field. He then went to Otis Air Force Base in Massachusetts, where he was promoted to major.

Major James attended the Air Command and Staff College at Maxwell Air Force Base in Alabama. After graduating in June 1957, he was assigned to air force headquarters in Washington, D.C. Three years later, he was sent to the Royal Air Force Station at Bentwaters, England, where he directed operations of the Eighty-first Tactical Fighter Wing and commanded the Ninety-second Tactical Fighter Squadron. Posted back to the United States, from 1964 to 1966 he directed operations of the 4453d Combat Crew Training Wing at Davis-Monthan Air Force Base in Arizona.

After serving with distinction in Vietnam, James was appointed vice-commander of the Thirty-third Tactical Fighter Wing at Elgin Air

THE WING COMMANDER

During the Vietnam War, in 1967, Chappie James was based in Thailand, where he served as wing commander. He flew seventy-eight combat missions over North Vietnam. On one of those missions, the planes in his command downed seven enemy Mig 21s, the highest enemy casualty rate of the war. For his part in that and other missions, he was awarded the Distinguished Flying Cross with two oak leaf clusters and the Air Medal with ten oak leaf clusters.

Force Base in Florida. Subsequently, he commanded Wheelus Air Force Base in Libya, North Africa, the largest American air base outside the United States. After a military takeover in Libya, James distinguished himself for handling relations with the new government.

By the time he received orders to report for a tour of duty as deputy assistant secretary of defense for public affairs at the Pentagon, U.S. military headquarters, in Washington, D.C., James had been promoted to general, with one star. In this position, one of his duties was to talk to college students who were protesting U.S. involvement in the Vietnam War. Shortly after National Guardsmen opened fire on protesting students at Kent State University in Ohio in 1970, killing several, James addressed an audience of students at the University of Florida. A white student shouted at him, "How can a black man like you defend the racist establishment?" James shot back, "Look, friend, I've been black fifty years, which is more than you will ever be, and I know what I believe in."[1]

General James believed in his country. During his four years at the Pentagon, he was elevated in rank from one-star to three-star general. He was then named vice-commander of the Military Airlift Command based at Scott Air Force Base in Illinois. Exactly one year later, on September 1, 1975, he received his fourth star and was named commander in chief of the North American Air Defense Command (NORAD), becoming the first black four-star general in U.S. military history, holding the highest post ever occupied by an African American.

In 1978, General Daniel "Chappie" James retired from the air force, having served for thirty-five years. Shortly afterward, he suffered a fatal heart attack in Colorado Springs, Colorado.

THE COMMANDER IN CHIEF

General James had a formidable mission—responsibility for the surveillance and defense of North American aerospace. His forces had to provide warning of any hostile attack on the North American continent by bombers and missiles. NORAD, headquartered in an underground bunker in Cheyenne Mountain in the Colorado Rockies, had a force of 63,000 and some of the most sophisticated weapons ever developed. James was prepared to use all the forces at his command, but his experience on the front lines of the domestic war between anti–Vietnam War protesters and the U.S. government had led him to believe, as he told an interviewer for the Colorado Springs *Sun,* that the most important weapon the United States could have was "not a physical one, it's a psychological one—a weapon called unity."[2]

◆ **Surveillance** is close observation of a person, group, or nation.

◆ **Aerospace** is earth's atmosphere and the space beyond.

A D M I R A L   S A M U E L   L.

GRAVELY Jr.

(B. 1922)

Samuel Lee Gravely Jr. was born on June 4, 1922, in the black section of Richmond, Virginia, the son of Samuel L. and Mary George Simon Gravely. Although he grew up under segregation, he was eager to take on the larger world. After graduating from Armstrong High School in Richmond, he entered Virginia Union University full of hope and ambition.

In September 1942, some nine months after the United States entered World War II, Gravely dropped out of college and enlisted in the U.S. Naval Reserve. Although he was accustomed to segregation, he resented the rigid separation of blacks at the Great Lakes Naval Training Station in Illinois. Black enlistees were confined to the separate Camp Robert Smalls (see Robert Smalls's story on page 60).

Clearly intelligent and determined to succeed, Gravely was chosen for officer training. At the University of California at Los Angeles, he was assigned, alone, to a basement room. He then attended midshipman school at Columbia University in New York City, and was the first black ensign commissioned in World War II. But among the

1,000 men who graduated from that program, he was also one of the few who was not given sea duty.

"You came to realize that you were saving America for democracy," he told an interviewer for *Ebony* in 1977, "but not allowed to participate in the g——d—— thing."[1]

Sent back to the Great Lakes Naval Training Station as an assistant battalion commander, he trained black troops. He found the segregation there even more difficult to handle. As a trainee, he had at least been assigned a bunk. But as a new officer, he was told there were no quarters available. Only whites could live in the bachelor officers' quarters.

In the spring of 1945, Gravely finally received a sea assignment, reporting as the first black officer to serve on the sub-chaser USS *PC-1264*, which along with the *Mason*, a destroyer escort, had been commissioned and designated specifically to train black crews. The ship was headed to Key West, Florida, when it radioed ahead for a berth. After an unusually long delay, the radioed reply cautioned that the "Negro officer aboard" would not be able to enter the officers' club.[2]

Released from active duty in April 1946, Gravely returned to Virginia Union and earned his B.A. But the navy had gotten into his blood. When the conflict between North and South Korea started heating up, Gravely was recalled to active duty. He decided to give the navy another try and returned to the service in August 1949.

Even though integration in the military was now official policy, and even though Secretary of the Navy James Forrestal was especially committed to integration, Gravely found that little had changed. There were as few blacks as possible on any one ship. Black officers were assigned to large ships only, not to submarines or destroyers. When Gravely reported to the USS *Iowa* in 1952, he accidentally discovered that although he was publicly welcomed, few fellow officers wanted to room with him.

HEAR! HEAR!
HOW OUR BROTHERS
Died For Freedom
AND HOW WE ARE CARRYING
ON THE FIGHT IN MISSISSIPPI

Mickey Schwerner   James Chaney   Andrew Goodman

HEAR
Mrs. Fanny Chaney
Courageous Mother of James Chaney
At New Zion Baptist Church
2319 THIRD STREET
THURS., AUG. 27, 1964
7:30 P. M.
CORE

While Samuel L. Gravely was standing up to segregation inside the military, the modern civil rights movement was born. This flyer honors three civil rights workers slain in the struggle in Mississippi.

Nevertheless, Gravely moved ahead and built his career. In Korea, he was assigned to the USS *Toledo* as communications officer and assistant operations officer. In July 1955, he was assigned to headquarters, Third Naval District, New York, as assistant district security officer. Along the way, he became the first black line officer to earn the rank of captain and then lieutenant.

Assigned first to the post of executive officer of the USS *Theodore E. Chandler*, Gravely became the navy's first black warship commander in February 1961. Less than a year later, he commanded the radar picket destroyer escort USS *Falgout*, based at Pearl Harbor, Hawaii. He fell in love with Hawaii and bought a home there. He and his wife, Alma Bernice Clark, raised their three children in Hawaii.

Gravely understood that there was always more to learn. From August 1963 to June 1964, he studied at the Naval War College in Newport, Rhode Island. Four years later, in June 1968, he was assigned to the Navy Satellite Communications Program, Office of the Assistant Chief, Naval Operations, in Washington, D.C. Two years after that, he took command of one of the navy's most modern guided missile frigates, the USS *Jouett*.

◆ A **frigate** is a warship that is smaller than a destroyer and is used for escort, anti-submarine, and patrol duties.

On June 2, 1971, the first black U.S. naval officer became the first black admiral in the navy. Two years later, Gravely became commander, Cruiser Destroyer Flotilla Two. Under his command were thirty ships, another first for African Americans in the navy.

By 1977, Admiral Gravely was in command of the United States Third Fleet in the Eastern Pacific, one of the navy's four fleets. This, of course, was also a black first. But when Gravely spoke to fellow officers or other audiences, he was a navy man first. His message was colorblind: "Pride in ourselves! Pride in our ships! And pride in our Navy!"[3]

Gravely was posted to Washington, D.C., in 1978 to direct the Defense Communications Agency. He retired on August 1, 1980.

BRIGADIER GENERAL
HAZEL W.
JOHNSON

(B. 1927)

Born in West Chester, Pennsylvania, in 1927, Hazel Johnson completed basic nurses' training at Harlem Hospital in 1950 and then worked as a nurse for five years. In 1955, her interest in travel spurred her to enlist in the army. By the time Hazel Johnson entered the Army Nurse Corps, she faced no legal or institutional barriers to her rise in the ranks.

Nurse Johnson had a plan for her life. She took advantage of the education provided by the military and earned a bachelor's degree in nursing from Villanova University in Pennsylvania in 1959. On graduation, she received a direct commission as a first lieutenant in the United States Army Nursing Corps.

Johnson continued her education as she was posted to various bases, earning a master of science in nursing education from Columbia University in 1963 and a Ph.D. in education administration through Catholic University in 1977.

In 1976, Jimmy Carter of Georgia was elected president of the United States. His secretary of the army, Clark Clifford, was

BLAZING A TRAIL

Hazel Johnson could thank nurse Mabel Keaton Staupers for blazing a trail for her to follow. A native of Barbados, in the West Indies, Staupers had emigrated to the United States with her parents in 1903 at the age of thirteen. Staupers received her training at Freedman's Hospital in Washington, D.C., before accepting a job in 1934 as the leader of the National Association of Colored Graduate Nurses. African American nurses formed this organization because the American Nurses Association denied them membership.

Staupers launched a campaign to bring black nurses into the Armed Forces Nurse Corps. Staupers asked First Lady Eleanor Roosevelt to pressure the president and other political leaders to accept more blacks, and by 1945 both the army and the navy had agreed to open the door. On the civilian front, the American Nurses Association integrated in 1948. The following year, the National Association of Colored Graduate Nurses dissolved. Nurse Staupers had succeeded in her mission.

determined to integrate the upper echelons of the service with the highest percentage of blacks. The following year, Hazel Johnson was named a full colonel, becoming the highest-ranking black woman in the United States military.

Two years after that, in 1979, Johnson was serving as chief nurse for the Army Medical Command in Korea when she achieved two signal honors. She became the first African American woman ever promoted to the rank of brigadier general and also the first black Chief of the Army Nurse Corps.

Johnson retired from the army in 1983 and worked as the director of the government affairs division of the American Nursing Association, while serving as adjunct professor at the Georgetown University School of Nursing. A few years later, she married David B. Brown, changed her last name to Johnson-Brown, and became a professor of nursing at George Mason University in Fairfax, Virginia, not far from her home in Clifton, Virginia.

Brigadier General Johnson's retirement left a temporary void in the top female leadership of the army. There were only two other women generals, and both were white. There were no African American women generals in the other branches of the service for two more years. (See Sherian Cadoria's story on page 147.)

GENERAL COLIN L.
POWELL

(B. 1937)

Born on April 5, 1937, in Harlem, New York City, Colin Luther Powell was the second child and only son of Luther Theophilus and Maud Ariel Powell. The elder Powells had moved to New York from the British island of Jamaica in the 1920s. His parents gave their son's first name the British pronunciation, KAH-lin. But during World War II, after a U.S. Army Air Corps captain, Colin P. Kelly, was killed bombing a Japanese warship, Colin Powell's friends began to pronounce his name like that hero's: KOH-lin. Today, he uses that pronunciation.

Powell grew up in the Hunts Point section of the South Bronx in New York City, where his family moved when he was about three. It was an immigrant neighborhood, and Colin learned to speak Yiddish. He attended elementary school and high school in the Bronx. An average but indifferent student, he was well liked by his teachers and classmates and excelled in sports. Although his grades were not high, he was accepted at New York University, which was looking for minority applicants and which noted the high recommendations from his teachers concerning his character. Unfortunately, the Powells could

not afford the tuition at NYU, so Colin enrolled at the City College of the City University of New York, which was essentially free for city residents. He chose to major in geology.

During the second semester of his sophomore year, Colin Powell joined the Army ROTC. He did so because he liked the uniforms the cadets wore. But he soon found that he liked the sense of order the military brought to his life. Being in ROTC gave him the discipline to apply himself to his studies, and although it took him an extra semester, he graduated with his degree in geology. He also graduated at the top of his ROTC class and was commissioned a second lieutenant in the U.S. Army Infantry.

By the time Powell received his commission, the army was better integrated racially than the rest of U.S. society, and there was real potential for him to advance. His first posting was to West Germany, where the United States maintained a number of bases to protect Western Europe against the post–World War II Soviet threat. He enjoyed his first experience in a foreign country, and by the time he returned to the United States in 1960, he had decided to make his career in the army.

In 1962, Colin Powell married Alma Vivian Johnson, who was attending school in Boston and whom he had met on a blind date. Four months later, he was sent to Vietnam with the first team of U.S. military advisers dispatched to help President Ngo Dinh Diem of South Vietnam in his fight against the China–backed Communist government of North Vietnam. Even though he was serving in a noncombat role, Powell was wounded while on patrol close to enemy territory. He stepped on a North Vietnamese bamboo trap and was injured in the foot. He received the Purple Heart, the military's honor for soldiers wounded in action, as well as the Bronze Star.

On his second tour of duty in Vietnam, Powell was in a helicopter crash. Powell, who was himself unhurt, re-entered the helicopter four times to rescue wounded comrades. For his bravery, he was awarded

WHAT DOES IT TAKE TO BE A LEADER?

Writing in his autobiography, *My American Journey*, General Powell said this about being a leader:

"The battalions that did best were those with the best commanders. A good commander could motivate his men to excel under any conditions. 'We're gonna win even if they give us one lousy round [of ammunition]' was the winning attitude. . . . Leadership is the art of accomplishing more than the science of management says is possible."[1]

the Bronze Star and Soldier's Medal. Altogether, he won eleven medals and decorations in Vietnam.

Powell then took advantage of army opportunities to get a graduate degree while in the service and enrolled at George Washington University in Washington, D.C. He enjoyed being with his young family, which by this time included a son and a daughter. In 1971, he earned his master's degree in business administration and then applied for a White House fellowship. He was one of seventeen Fellows chosen from 1,500 military and civilian applicants. Powell went to work in the Office of Management and Budget for the year. After his year as a White House Fellow, he returned to active duty, serving as a battalion commander in South Korea.

The following year, he was rotated home to a staff job at the Pentagon, the headquarters of all the U.S. military services, promoted to full colonel, and made chief military aide to the special assistant to the secretary of defense. Over the next three years, he held other deputy and assistant positions. He also enrolled at the National War College and graduated with distinction. Promoted to brigadier general, he was named deputy commander at Fort Leavenworth, Kansas.

At the Vietnam Veterans Memorial in 1991, General Colin L. Powell paid respect to the thousands who sacrificed their lives. Here he greets Corporal Patrick McGrath.

At Fort Leavenworth, Powell became interested in the history of the Buffalo Soldiers and suggested that a statue honoring them be erected at the fort. But he was soon recalled to Washington, D.C. The idea would have to wait.

President Ronald Reagan, who had been elected in 1980, had named Powell's old bosses at the Office of Management and Budget, Caspar Weinberger and Frank Carlucci, secretary and deputy secretary of defense, respectively. They wanted Powell on their staffs. He returned to Washington in 1983 to take up the job of keeping the White House and other departments informed of all military operations, and he did so with grace and humor that soon earned the respect of all those who came into contact with him. In 1987, when Frank Carlucci was named national security adviser, Powell was asked to be his deputy. He was the first African American to hold this position. Two years later, when Carlucci was named secretary of defense, Powell became the first African American head of the National Security Council. President Reagan also awarded him his fourth general's star.

President Reagan stepped down after serving two terms in office—the legal limit. His successor, former vice president George Bush, named his own national security adviser, and Colin Powell was scheduled to take over the United States Forces Command at Fort McPherson, Georgia, responsible for assigning U.S. troops around the world. But he and his wife, Alma, had just started to settle into their new life in Georgia when he received a call from President Bush, who wanted to name him chairman of the Joint Chiefs of Staff.

Created in 1947, just after the close of World War II, the Joint Chiefs of Staff consists of the four-star heads of the army, navy, marines, and air force, as well as a chairman. These five meet in secret session three times a week at the Pentagon to set the military policies of the United States and decide where the men and women in the U.S. armed forces are stationed throughout the world. The chairman of the Joint Chiefs of Staff commands the armed forces on behalf of the president of the United States and since 1986 has been the highest military official in the nation. At age fifty-two, Colin Powell was the youngest officer ever to serve in that position, and once again, he was the first African American.

Almost immediately, Powell was called upon to oversee U.S. response to a crisis in Panama, where a coup was

✦ A **coup** is the sudden overturning of a government.

staged against military dictator Manuel Noriega. Powell authorized an attempt by U.S. forces to capture Noriega, which failed. Then, with

THE HERO OF OPERATION DESERT STORM

On August 2, 1990, 80,000 Iraqi troops invaded Kuwait and quickly took control of that tiny, oil-rich nation. President Bush wanted to rescue Kuwait, and while Powell did not agree entirely with the president's policy of intervention in the Middle East, he planned and directed Operation Desert Storm—a large-scale bombing campaign, followed by a ground war against Iraq. The largest military movement in history, Operation Desert Storm was a joint effort of United States and United Nations troops that began on January 17, 1991, and ended in success with the rescue of Kuwait from Iraq's control at the end of February. General Colin Powell, and General H. Norman Schwarzkopf, commander of United Nations forces in the Persian Gulf War, were hailed as heroes and awarded specially struck gold medals ordered by President Bush.

the authorization of President Bush, he ordered the invasion of Panama, which resulted in Noriega's surrender and imprisonment in the United States and the re-establishment of peace in Panama. Meanwhile, another crisis occurred in the Philippines, where a military coup was attempted against President Corazon Aquino. Powell authorized U.S. forces to help Aquino and put down the rebellion.

As chairman of the Joint Chiefs of Staff, Powell now had the clout needed to push forward the idea of a monument to the Buffalo Soldiers at Fort Leavenworth, Kansas. The larger-than-life-size equestrian statue surrounded by pools and a waterfall was based on a painting entitled *Scout's Out*, by Lee Bubaker. Ground was broken in July 1990, with General Powell in attendance.

Speaking to the crowd of thousands that had gathered for the ceremony, Powell said, pointing to the statue, "There he is, the Buffalo Soldier, on horseback, in his coat of blue, eagles on his buttons, crossed sabers on his canteen, rifle in hand, pistol on his hip, brave, iron-willed, every bit the soldier that his white brother was. . . . I am deeply mindful of the debt I owe to those who went before me. . . . I challenge every young person here today; don't forget their service and their sacrifice. . . . Be eagles!"[2]

The president reappointed Powell early to a second two-year term as Chairman of the Joint Chiefs of Staff. In 1993, at the end of that term, Powell announced his retirement from the military to devote time to his family and to a new career as a writer and public speaker. In 1994, he was called upon by President Bill Clinton to help negotiate the return to power of Haiti's exiled president, Jean-Bertrand Aristide. Perceived as a man of immense personal integrity, Powell was suggested as a strong candidate for president or vice president in the 1996 election. But General Powell, who had kept his political opinions to himself throughout his military career, chose not to enter politics. His autobiography, *My American Journey*, was published in 1995.

BRIGADIER GENERAL
SHERIAN
CADORIA

(B. 1940)

Most African American women who achieved high rank in the United States Army, such as Hazel Johnson-Brown, rose through the nursing corps. Sherian Cadoria was the first African American woman army general to rise through a traditional male unit.

Born in Marksville, Louisiana, the youngest of three children, Sherian Grace Cadoria was raised in a close-knit family headed by her mother, Bernice, who emphasized devout Catholic faith and hard work. Determined to be helpful on the family farm, Sherian was dragging 50-pound bags of cotton at the age of three. She also worked hard at school. After high school, she attended Southern University and earned a degree in business education.

Cadoria entered the army in 1961, at a time when opportunities for African American men were opening up. Sexism, however, was still a dominant force in the service, limiting women to certain roles. Cadoria encountered more problems because of her gender than because of her race.

You Have to Prove Yourself

General Cadoria did not regret having chosen a career in the army. "A woman today can excel in the army," she told an interviewer for *Ebony* magazine in 1985. "So many doors have been knocked down." But she added that women still had to prove themselves much more than men: "You have to prove that you can do the job many times better than your male counterparts. . . . [But] as women work alongside their male counterparts, they'll recognize that we have the ability and that we can do quality work. And things will change. Maybe not in my lifetime, but it's coming."[1]

The United States was beginning to get involved in the conflict in Vietnam when she entered the Army. Cadoria interviewed for a job as a protocol officer in Vietnam, whose job was to escort various military and civilian officials and see to their needs. The colonel who interviewed her stated at the outset that the only reason he was talking to her was because he was forced to. He said that women were not strong enough to carry the visitors' luggage. Cadoria informed him that as a child she had hefted 50-pound sacks of cotton; but the colonel remained unconvinced and Cadoria did not get the job.

♦ **Protocols** are sets of rules that govern the behaviors and procedures within the military.

Cadoria eventually did secure a job as a protocol officer in the Qui Nhom Support Command in South Vietnam, escorting important visitors. When off-duty, she began working with the Dominican nuns stationed in the area, visiting hospitals and leper colonies. The human toll of the war affected her deeply, and she began to seriously consider becoming a nun. After three months, however, the priest with whom she worked advised her that her true calling was working with soldiers.

After her tour of duty in Vietnam, Cadoria was posted back to the United States, to a position with the Military Police at Fort McClellan, Alabama, where she became the first woman to command the otherwise all-male Military Police Training Battalion. Over the next several years, she served at posts in the United States and in Europe and rose steadily in the ranks, racking up other "firsts": first woman brigade commander of the First Regional Criminal Investigation Command; first woman chief of the Office of Army Law Enforcement; first black woman to attend the U.S. Army Command and General Staff College, the National Defense University Institute of Higher Studies, and the U.S. Army War College.

In the spring of 1985, Sherian Cadoria was awarded a general's star, the first as a line officer. Shortly afterward, in July 1985, Brigadier General Cadoria was assigned to the Pentagon in Washington, D.C., where she directed the manpower and personnel division of the organization of the Joint Chiefs of Staff. In that position, she was responsible for advising the Joint Chiefs on the needs and effective uses of personnel for all branches of the armed services. She also supervised the evaluation of U.S. military operations throughout the world.

Until 1973, women in the army were denied the right to have children, but Sherian Cadoria's decisions not to marry and have children were her own. She was godmother to many children around the world and regarded her soldiers as her children. She retired in 1990 as the highest-ranking African American woman in the U.S. armed forces. She became a full-time speaker, lecturer, and consultant.

COLONEL GUION S.
BLUFORD JR.

(B. 1942)

Guion Stewart Bluford Jr., the first African American in space, was born in Philadelphia, Pennsylvania, on November 22, 1942. His father was a mechanical engineer, and his mother taught special education classes in the Philadelphia public school system. Guion, whose name is pronounced GUY-on, and who always preferred to be called Guy, took an early interest in how things work. He was especially interested in airplanes and built model airplanes as a boy, curious about how the craft moved through the air.

Bluford was fifteen years old and in high school when the Soviet Union launched *Sputnik 1*, the first craft to go into space. The world immediately recognized that space was a new frontier to conquer, and the United States worried that if it did not act to encourage greater advancements in science and math, the Soviet Union would outdistance it in what came to be called the "space race." The administration of President Dwight D. Eisenhower urged the nation's schools to emphasize math and science and encouraged the nation's students to study and excel in those subjects.

Guy Bluford was fascinated with *Sputnik 1* and excited about the possibilities of space travel and exploration. By the time he was a senior at Overbrook High School in Philadelphia, he had decided he wanted to be an aerospace engineer. But he received no encouragement to pursue such a career. His white guidance counselor at Overbrook apparently did not think that the new national push for excellence in math and science applied to a black student like Guion Bluford. The guidance counselor told Bluford he was not college material and suggested that he attend a technical school after high school graduation. There, Bluford might learn to be an automotive mechanic, but he certainly would not become an aerospace engineer.

Bluford paid little attention to that guidance counselor. It was a given that he would go to college. His parents both had master's degrees, and their parents before them had college degrees. Guion Bluford Jr. was going to college, too. He applied to several colleges and was accepted into the aerospace engineering program at Pennsylvania State University, where he entered in the fall of 1960, one of only 400 African Americans in a student population of several thousand.

At Penn State, Bluford joined the campus Air Force Reserve Officers Training Corps (ROTC) because he had his sights set on joining the air force after graduation. In the summer after his junior year, he attended boot camp at Otis Air National Guard Base in Cape Cod, Massachusetts, and had his first ride in an air force plane. He decided that knowing how to fly aircraft would make him a better aerospace engineer.

Bluford married Linda Tull, a fellow student at Penn State, while they were both still in college. Their first child, a son whom they named Guion III, was born in June 1964, one month after Bluford graduated from Penn State with his B.S. degree as well as the ROTC's Distinguished Graduate Award. Bluford went into the air force immediately and moved his family to Arizona, where he underwent pilot training at Williams Air Force Base. He received his pilot's wings in 1965 and then began a tour of duty in Vietnam.

By that time, the United States had become deeply involved on the side of South Vietnam in its civil war with the communist-backed regime of North Vietnam. Bluford served with the 557th Tactical Fighter Squadron based in Cam Ranh Bay, South Vietnam, flying F-4 and F-4C Phantom jets. Altogether, during his service in Vietnam, he flew 144 combat missions, 65 of them over enemy territory in North Vietnam. He also collected ten air force medals. But he missed the birth of his second son, James T.

On his return from Vietnam, Bluford was assigned to teach cross-country and acrobatic flying at Sheppard Air Force Base in Texas. But Bluford held on to his dream of becoming an aerospace engineer and was accepted in 1972 at the Air Force Institute of Technology. Two years later, he received his master's degree in aerospace engineering. He then began taking courses toward his doctoral degree while working at the Air Force Flight Dynamics Laboratory at Wright-Patterson Air Force Base in Ohio. There, he tested new aircraft and aircraft designs and developed plans for aircraft based on the latest discoveries in aerodynamics. A special computer program he developed to calculate air pressure, density, and velocity on any part of a delta (triangular) wing of an aircraft became the basis for his Ph.D. dissertation.

By the time Bluford received his doctorate in aerospace engineering, he had decided that he wanted to be an astronaut. He had followed with great interest and excitement the achievements of the United States in space—its first manned rocket in space in 1961, the first orbiting of Earth in a manned spacecraft in 1962, the landing on the moon in 1969, followed by a number of successes with unmanned spacecraft in the early 1970s. The focus of NASA (National Aeronautics and Space Administration) was now on the space shuttle, a reusable craft designed to do practical work in space, and each year a few men were accepted into the shuttle astronaut program. Bluford knew that he faced tough competition; in the year he applied, so did more than 8,850 others.

Among those accepted by NASA in 1978 was the first woman, Dr. Sally K. Ride. Three black men were also accepted—Dr. Ronald McNair, Charles F. Bolden, and Guion S. Bluford. They were not the first black men in the astronaut program. In 1967, Air Force Major Robert Lawrence had joined the astronaut program; but he had died in a tragic airplane accident later that same year.

Bluford moved his family to Houston, Texas, close to the Johnson Space Flight Center, where he and the other new astronauts attended "shuttle school" for a year, at the end of which he became a full-fledged astronaut. He and his fellow astronauts then went to work in the program, preparing for the first shuttle flight.

The first shuttle, *Columbia*, was launched in 1981 and completed its fourth mission in July 1982. The second shuttle, *Challenger*, went up in April 1983, and on its second flight, in June, Dr. Sally K. Ride was aboard as a mission specialist. On its third mission, on August 30, 1983, Dr. Guion S. Bluford Jr. became the first African American in space. Although he was a qualified pilot, he had joined the shuttle program as a mission specialist, and he was in charge of deploying a communications and weather satellite for the nation of India.

Over the next decade, Bluford continued in the shuttle program and went into space three more times. He was a mission specialist aboard *Challenger* on October 30, 1985, the first mission to carry a crew of eight—the largest crew to fly in space and one that included three Europeans. He served as a mission specialist aboard *Discovery* twice, in April–May 1991 and in December 1992. Following his retirement from the shuttle program, Bluford went to work for NYMA, Inc., in Greenbelt, Maryland. The company, which Bluford joined as vice president and general manager of the engineering division, provides scientific engineering and technical support services to government and commercial clients.

Although Colonel Guion S. Bluford Jr. paved the way, it was not long before other African Americans went into space. Dr. Ronald

THE FIRST IN SPACE

Many famous blacks were on hand at Cape Canaveral, Florida, to see the first African American go up in space. Comedian and television star Bill Cosby put the event in perspective when he said, "Our race is one which has been quite qualified for a long time. The people who have allowed Guy to make this mission are the ones who have passed the test."[1]

During the weeklong mission—the first to have a night launch and a night landing—Bluford deployed the satellite for India and otherwise contributed to the mission's success. But he was more than just a member of the crew—he was a "first." When President Ronald Reagan called to congratulate all the members of the crew, he had a special message for Bluford, that he was "making it plain that we are in an era of brotherhood here in our land."[2] After the shuttle landed at Edwards Air Force Base in California, Bluford was besieged with requests for photographs and interviews. When, after a time, the attention died down, he was relieved to be just another astronaut again.

McNair, a civilian with no military service who had entered the program at the same time as Bluford, was aboard the shuttle *Challenger* when its equipment failed and it blew up shortly after takeoff on January 28, 1986, killing everyone on board. In November 1989, Air Force Colonel Frederick D. Gregory, who had also joined the shuttle program in 1978, was the mission commander aboard the shuttle *Discovery*—the first African American mission commander. In March 1992, aboard *Atlantis,* the mission commander was another African American, Colonel Charles F. Bolden, a graduate of the United States Naval Academy at Annapolis, Maryland. Late in September of that same year, the first African American woman was launched into space: Dr. Mae C. Jemison, a physician and chemical engineer who had entered the shuttle program as a civilian.

COMMANDER
ROBERT O.
GOODMAN JR.

(B. 1956)

Robert O. Goodman Jr. was born into the military life. His father, Robert O. Goodman Sr., was one of the first high-ranking black officers in the air force. The elder Goodman and his wife Marilyn were stationed at Ramey Air Force Base in Puerto Rico, when Robert Jr. was born in 1956. Before Robert Jr. was three years old, he had lived on military facilities in Florida, Texas, and Massachusetts. Two more sons were born, and when Goodman Sr. was assigned to Pease Air Force Base in Newington, New Hampshire, the family settled in nearby Portsmouth, where Robert Jr. attended public schools.

Robert Jr., who received the nickname "Goody" early on, grew up in a largely white community and was well liked. According to his father, Robert's slight build spurred him to be a strong competitor who was unhappy being anything but number one.[1]

While in the tenth grade at Portsmouth High School, Robert fell in love with Terry Lynn Bryant, the daughter of a naval shipyard worker. A quiet, self-possessed young woman, Terry Lynn rejected the

standard scruffy blue jeans uniform that most students wore and took special care with her wardrobe.

Robert had been determined from an early age to become a pilot, and in 1974, there were no barriers to living his dream. In his senior year at Portsmouth High School, he sought and secured appointments to the U.S. Naval Academy at Annapolis, Maryland, the Merchant Marine Academy, and the U.S. Military Academy at West Point, New York. He chose to attend Annapolis. His two younger brothers would also choose military careers, one in the Coast Guard and the other in the navy. On graduation from Portsmouth High School, Robert went off to Annapolis. On January 6, 1976, a little more than a year after he entered Annapolis, Robert and Terry Lynn were married, and she joined him in Maryland. A daughter, Tina, was born about a year later.

Goodman embarked on an exciting, successful career. He graduated from the academy in 1978 and was assigned to the Naval Recruiting District in Boston. Seven months later, he began flight training at the Naval Aviation Schools Command in Pensacola, Florida. He received his navy flier's wings in August 1981, carrying on a tradition begun by Jesse L. Brown (1926–1950), the first African American to earn a naval aviator's wings and who was killed in Korea while on a combat mission in 1950. Goodman subsequently joined Attack Squadron Eighty-five at Oceana Naval Air Station in Virginia Beach, Virginia, as a navigator-bombardier. There, his and Terry's second daughter, Morgan, was born.

As a navy pilot, Goodman had to be prepared for war and conflict. By the time he earned his flier's wings, a long-simmering situation in the Middle East was especially tense. U.S. peacekeeping forces in Beirut, Lebanon, were coming under attack. At the same time, the United States decided to invade the Caribbean island of Grenada. In October 1983, when many of the U.S. warplanes used in the Middle East were diverted to Grenada, Goodman was sent to Lebanon. In 1983, Syrian aircraft based in Lebanon began attacking U.S.

reconnaissance flights. In retaliation, on December 4, the United States undertook an air strike against Syrian aircraft positions in Lebanon. Twenty-eight American planes were sent out on that retaliatory strike. Among those ordered into action were Lieutenant Mark O. Lange, a pilot from Fraser, Michigan, and his navigator-bombardier, Robert O. Goodman Jr.

Flying into the sunrise, and thus forced to come in low over the mountains, Lange and Goodman's A-6E Intruder jet took a direct hit from enemy anti-aircraft guns and crashed. Goodman and Lange ejected and parachuted to the ground, where Lange was killed by ground fire. Goodman managed to land safely, suffering minor injuries in the process. A single-pilot A-7 aircraft was also downed by Syrian anti-aircraft fire. Its pilot was rescued.

In Goodman's recollection, he blacked out after ejecting from his aircraft and awoke to find that his hands were bound so tightly that his fingers were numb. The Syrians had stripped him of his clothes, except for his underwear and a T-shirt. They had placed a bag over his head so he could not see where he was. He was locked in a dank basement cell and was subjected to occasional beatings and interrogation. Sensing that his captors aimed to scare him rather than to hurt him, Goodman gave vague answers to their questions. The beatings stopped altogether after International Red Cross workers visited him on December 8 to ascertain how he was being treated.

Goodman prepared himself as best he could for a long period of incarceration. He was fortunate that his captivity lasted less than a month, thanks to an unexpected turn of events. The Reverend Jesse Jackson was then campaigning for the Democratic nomination for president of the United States. He knew that he faced an uphill battle, not just because he was black but also because critics charged that he had no experience in international relations. Jackson saw an opportunity to show his statesmanship by securing Goodman's freedom.

With Louis Farrakhan, national minister of the Nation of Islam, and an entourage of other blacks, Jackson flew to Damascus, Syria, late in December. The group first met with Syria's foreign minister, Abdel Halim Khaddam, who told the black leaders that while Syria respected their efforts, it was in a state of war alert and that letting Goodman go would damage the morale of Syrian soldiers.

On New Year's Eve, Jackson and his entourage were allowed to meet with Goodman, with whom they then appeared before television cameras. Goodman seemed stunned by the bright television lights at first, but he soon relaxed. Jackson assured Goodman that he would do all he could to secure his release, and Goodman held on to that hope as he was led back to his cell.

The following day, Jackson and his delegation finally met with Hafiz al-Assad, Syria's president. Jackson appealed to Assad, saying, "It is important that you take the leap of faith and break the cycle of pain and return that boy to his parents and leave a good taste in the mouth of the American people."[2] Assad would say only that he would call a meeting of his advisers and reconsider Goodman's case.

The following morning, Jackson met again with Khaddam, who informed him of the decision to release Goodman to him. Later that day, Goodman, Jackson, and his entourage boarded a U.S. Air Force C-141 cargo transport plane bound for West Germany.

From there, they flew back to the United States, where Goodman was reunited with his family at Andrews Air Force Base near Washington, D.C. He was then hospitalized for the knee injury he had sustained during his bailout from the crippled A-6 jet. His wife and daughters later attended a welcome-home celebration in his honor at Portsmouth High School, where the Reverend Jesse Jackson was also honored. Goodman did not attend because navy regulations barred him from political occasions.

New Hampshire just happened to be the site of the first presidential primary in the election year of 1985, and candidate Jesse Jackson could not have asked for a happier coincidence. But although he did well in New Hampshire, he failed to win the Democratic presidential nomination the following summer.

Goodman, who had been uncomfortable in the limelight, was happy to return to his life in the navy. Grounded for some months because of his injury, he entered the Naval Postgraduate School in Monterey, California, in May 1985. Elevated to the rank of lieutenant commander in November 1987, he was posted to the USS *America*, a naval aircraft carrier.

In July 1992, Goodman was assigned to U.S. Space Command headquarters at Pease Air Force Base in Colorado. Fifteen months later, he was promoted to commander.

CHRONOLOGY

1750	Peter Salem born
1753	Lemuel Haynes born
1760	Deborah Sampson born
1770	Boston Massacre
1775	Battles of Lexington and Concord, Massachusetts, begin the Revolutionary War
	Battle of Bunker Hill
1776	Declaration of Independence issued
	General George Washington crosses the Delaware River into New Jersey
1777	Battle of Saratoga
1781	British General Cornwallis surrenders at Yorktown, ending the Revolutionary War
1783	Treaty of Paris formally recognizes the new United States of America
1792	John Bathan Vashon born
1794	William Goyens born
1804	Lemuel Haynes is the first black person to receive an honorary degree from a white college in the United States
1812	Martin Robison Delany born
	War of 1812 between the United States and Great Britain begins
1815	Peter Vogelsang born
	War of 1812 ends
1816	Peter Salem dies
1820	Harriet Tubman born
1821	Liberia, on the coast of West Africa, is established by the American Colonization Society
1827	Deborah Sampson dies
1833	Lemuel Haynes dies
1835	Texas Revolution breaks out
1836	Texas declares its independence
1837	Pinckney Benton Stewart Pinchback born
1839	Robert Smalls born
	Michael A. Healy born

c. 1840	Christian A. Fleetwood born
	William H. Carney born
1840s	The term Underground Railroad comes into use
1845	Texas admitted to the Union as the twenty-eighth state
1846	Mexican War begins
1848	Mexican War ends
1849	George Washington Williams born
1854	John Bathan Vashon dies
1856	Henry O. Flipper born
	William Goyens dies
1860	Abraham Lincoln of Illinois elected president of the United States
1861	Seven southern states secede from the Union and form the Confederate States of America; the Civil War begins
1862	Robert Smalls hijacks the Confederate *Planter* and delivers her to the Union navy
1863	President Abraham Lincoln issues the Emancipation Proclamation freeing slaves in the secessionist Confederate States of America
	Fifty-fourth Massachusetts Volunteer Regiment mustered into service
	Fifty-fourth Massachusetts Volunteer Regiment assaults Fort Wagner, South Carolina
1864	Charles A. Young born
1865	Martin R. Delany is the first black man to receive a regular army commission
	The Civil War ends
	Reconstruction begins
1866	Congress authorizes the first peacetime units of African American soldiers; the Ninth and Tenth Cavalries are nicknamed the Buffalo Soldiers
1867	United States purchases Alaska from Russia
1869–1878	Indian Campaigns
1871	Pinckney Benton Stewart Pinchback succeeds to the post of lieutenant governor of Reconstruction Louisiana
1872–1873	For forty-two days, P. B. S. Pinchback serves as acting governor of Louisiana
1876	Robert Smalls elected to Congress; reelected in 1878, 1880, and 1882, he serves longer than any other black congressman of the period

1877	Benjamin O. Davis Sr. born
	Henry O. Flipper is the first black to graduate from the United States Military Academy at West Point
	Reconstruction ends
1879	The United States Navy is given charge of the Alaska territory
1885	Martin Robison Delany dies
1887	Peter Vogelsang dies
1891	George Washington Williams dies
1897	Henry Johnson born
	A monument to Colonel Robert Gould Shaw and the men of the all-black Fifty-fourth Massachusetts Volunteer Regiment is erected on Boston Common
1898	Spanish-American War
	First Lieutenant Charles A. Young of the Ninth Ohio Volunteer Infantry, an African American unit, is said to be the first black officer to command a battalion in the army
1900	William H. Carney is the first African American to be awarded the Congressional Medal of Honor; cited for valor in the Fifty-fourth Massachusetts's assault on Fort Wagner in 1863, Carney does not receive the medal until thirty-seven years later
1904	Michael A. Healy dies
	Colonel Charles A. Young is the first African American U.S. military attaché, assigned to Haiti and Santo Domingo
1908	William H. Carney dies
1911	Captain Charles A. Young achieves the rank of major, the highest rank of any black officer in the army, except for chaplains
1912	Benjamin O. Davis Jr. born
1913	Harriet Tubman dies
1914	World War I begins in Europe
1915	Robert Smalls dies
1917	United States enters World War I
1918	The 369th Infantry is the first American negro unit in battle in World War I
	Henry Johnson and Needham Roberts are the first American soldiers in the war to receive individually the Croix de Guerre, France's highest honor for bravery in action
	The 364th Infantry is the first Allied unit to enter Germany
	World War I ends
	Charity Adams Earley born

1919	Dorie Miller born
	Vernon J. Baker born
1920	Daniel "Chappie" James Jr. born
1921	Pinckney Benton Stewart Pinchback dies
1922	Samuel L. Gravely Jr. born
	Charles A. Young dies
1927	Hazel W. Johnson born
1929	Henry Johnson dies
	Camp No. 24, National Indian War Veterans, in Washington, D.C., is the first all-black army camp
1937	Colin L. Powell born
1939	World War II begins in Europe
1940	Henry O. Flipper dies
	Benjamin O. Davis Sr. promoted to brigadier general, the first African American general since the Reconstruction period and the first ever African American general in the regular army
	U.S. Army Air Corps establishes an Advanced Army Flying School for blacks at Tuskegee Institute
1940	Sherian Cadoria born
1941	The U.S. Army forms the Women's Army Auxiliary Corps (WAAC)
	Japanese planes bomb U.S. Navy at Pearl Harbor, Hawaii, on December 7, and the United States enters World War II on the side of the Allies
1942	Guion S. Bluford Jr. born
	Mess Attendant Dorie Miller awarded the Navy Cross
1943	Dorie Miller dies
	Congress converts the WAAC into the Women's Army Corps (WAC), part of the regular army
	Allied forces invade Italy
	The Ninety-ninth Pursuit Squadron, made up of airmen trained at Tuskegee and under the command of Colonel Benjamin O. Davis Jr., is sent to North Africa
1945	Colonel Benjamin O. Davis Jr. awarded the Distinguished Flying Cross
	Vernon J. Baker is the most highly decorated black American soldier in the Mediterranean theater
	Germany surrenders and World War II in Europe ends
	Japan surrenders and World War II in the Pacific ends

1948	President Harry S. Truman signs Executive Order 9981 establishing equality of treatment and opportunity for all persons in the armed services
	Congress passes the Armed Services Integration Act
1949	The 332d Fighter Wing is the first all-black unit to be integrated into the United States Air Force
1950	Korean War begins
1953	Korean War ends
1954	Integration of the United States armed forces is completed
	Vietnam divided into North Vietnam and South Vietnam; war soon breaks out
1956	Robert O. Goodman Jr. born
1957	The Soviet Union launches *Sputnik 1* into space
1959	Alaska admitted to the Union as the forty-ninth state
1961	First American military support troops arrive to assist South Vietnam; the Vietnam War is the first in which U.S. forces are totally integrated
	Lieutenant Samuel L. Gravely is the U.S. Navy's first black warship commander
1967	Air Force Major Robert Lawrence is the first African American to join the astronaut program of the National Aeronautics and Space Administration (NASA)
1970	Benjamin O. Davis Sr. dies
1971	Samuel L. Gravely is the first black admiral in the U.S. Navy
1973	Vietnam War ends
1975	General Daniel "Chappie" James receives his fourth star and is named commander in chief of the North American Air Defense Command, becoming the first black four-star general in United States military history and holding the highest post ever occupied by an African American
1977	Admiral Samuel L. Gravely is the first African American to command one of the navy's four fleets, the United States Third Fleet in the Eastern Pacific
	Hazel W. Johnson is named a full colonel, becoming the highest-ranking black woman in the United States military
1978	Daniel "Chappie" James Jr. dies
	African Americans Dr. Guion S. Bluford Jr., Dr. Ronald McNair, and Charles F. Bolden are accepted into the NASA astronaut program

1979	Hazel W. Johnson is first African American woman promoted to the rank of brigadier general and also the first black Chief of the Army Nurse Corps
1980	Hazel W. Johnson is promoted to full colonel, becoming the highest-ranking black woman in the United States military
1983	On the third mission of the space shuttle *Challenger,* Dr. Guion S. Bluford Jr. becomes the first African American in space
	Syrian aircraft based in Lebanon attack American reconaissance flights. In retaliation, the United States undertakes an air strike against Syrian aircraft positions in Lebanon; Navy Lieutenant Robert O. Goodman Jr.'s plane is shot down, and he is captured
1984	The Syrians release Lieutenant Robert O. Goodman Jr. to the Reverend Jesse Jackson
1985	Sherian Cadoria is awarded a general's star; she is the first African American woman line officer to be promoted to this rank
1987	Colin Powell is awarded his fourth general's star; he is the first African American head of the National Security Council
1989	General Colin Powell is the first African American chairman of the Joint Chiefs of Staff
	General Colin Powell orders U.S. troops to the Philippines to assist President Corazon Aquino in fighting off a coup attempt
	On orders of President George Bush, General Colin Powell carries out Operation Just Cause, the American invasion of Panama, the first decisive victory for American forces since World War II
1990	Ground is broken for a monument to the Buffalo Soldiers at Fort Leavenworth, Kansas
	Iraq invades its neighbor Kuwait
1991	Generals Colin L. Powell, H. Norman Schwarzkopf, and others plan and execute Operation Desert Storm against Iraq, forcing Iraq to withdraw from Kuwait
1997	Vernon J. Baker awarded the Congressional Medal of Honor; six other black veterans of World War II are awarded the honor posthumously
1998	A memorial to the United States Colored Troops in the Civil War is dedicated in Washington, D.C.

NOTES

INTRODUCTION

1. Colin L. Powell. *My American Journey* (New York: Random House, 1995), 114.

PRIVATE PETER SALEM

1. Sidney Kaplan. *The Black Presence in the Era of the American Revolution, 1770–1800* (New York: New York Graphic Society, 1973), 18.

PRIVATE AUSTIN DABNEY

1. Sidney Kaplan. *The Black Presence in the Era of the American Revolution, 1770–1800* (New York: New York Graphic Society, 1973), 52.
2. Ibid.

PRIVATE LEMUEL HAYNES

1. Sidney Kaplan. *The Black Presence in the Era of the American Revolution, 1770–1800* (New York: New York Graphic Society, 1973), 103.
2. Ibid.
3. Robert Ewell Greene. *Black Defenders of America, 1775–1973* (Chicago: Johnson Publishing, 1974), 13.
4. Sidney Kaplan. *The Black Presence in the Era of the American Revolution, 1770–1800* (New York: New York Graphic Society, 1973), 105.

DEBORAH SAMPSON

1. Jessie Carney Smith, ed. *Epic Lives: One Hundred Black Women Who Made a Difference* (Detroit: Visible Ink Press, 1993), 974.
2. Ibid., 975.

WILLIAM GOYENS

1. William Loren Katz. *The Black West: A Documentary and Pictorial History* (Garden City, N.Y.: Doubleday, 1971), 63.

MAJOR MARTIN ROBISON DELANY

1. Waldo E. Martin Jr. *The Mind of Frederick Douglass* (Chapel Hill: University of North Carolina Press, 1984), 95.
2. Ira Berlin, ed. *Freedom: A Documentary History of Emancipation 1861–1867. Series II: The Black Military Experience* (New York: Cambridge University Press, 1982), 102.
3. Robert Ewell Greene. *Black Defenders of America, 1775–1973* (Chicago: Johnson Publishing, 1974), 121.

LIEUTENANT PETER VOGELSANG

1. Peter Burchard. *"We'll Stand By the Union": Robert Gould Shaw and the Black 54th Massachusetts Regiment* (New York: Facts on File, 1993), 85.

2. James M. McPherson. *The Negro's Civil War* (New York: Ballantine, 1991), 195.

HARRIET TUBMAN

1. Patricia W. Romero, ed. *Reminiscences of My Life in Camp* (New York: M. Wiener, 1988).

GOVERNOR PINCKNEY BENTON STEWART PINCHBACK

1. James M. McPherson. *The Negro's Civil War* (New York: Ballantine, 1991), 189.

2. Jim Haskins. *America's First Black Governor: Pinckney Benton Stewart Pinchback* (Trenton, N.J.: Africa World Press, 1996), 25.

CONGRESSMAN ROBERT SMALLS

1. James M. McPherson. *The Negro's Civil War* (New York: Ballantine, 1991), 159.

SERGEANT MAJOR CHRISTIAN A. FLEETWOOD

1. Thomas Truxton Moebs. *Black Soldiers—Black Sailors—Black Ink* (Chesapeake Bay and Paris: Moebs Publishing, 1994), 241.

2. Robert Ewell Greene. *Black Defenders of America, 1775–1973* (Chicago: Johnson Publishing, 1974), 351.

3. Ibid.

SERGEANT WILLIAM H. CARNEY

1. Peter Burchard. *"We'll Stand By the Union": Robert Gould Shaw and the Black 54th Massachusetts Regiment* (New York: Facts On File, 1983), 92.

SERGEANT GEORGE WASHINGTON WILLIAMS

1. John Hope Franklin. *George Washington Williams, A Biography* (Chicago: University of Chicago Press, 1985), 3.

LIEUTENANT HENRY O. FLIPPER

1. John M. Carroll. *The Black Military Experience in the American West* (New York: Liveright Publishing, 1971), 348–349.

COLONEL CHARLES A. YOUNG

1. Frank N. Schubert. *On the Trail of the Buffalo Soldier: Biographies of African-Americans in the U.S. Army, 1866–1917* (Wilmington, Del.: Scholarly Resources, 1995), 490.
2. Ibid.
3. Ibid.

PRIVATE HENRY JOHNSON

1. Langston Hughes. *Famous Negro Heroes of America* (New York: Dodd, Mead & Company, 1958), 178.
2. Ibid., 177.

LIEUTENANT COLONEL CHARITY ADAMS EARLEY

1. Charity Adams Earley. *One Woman's Army: A Black Officer Remembers the WAC* (College Station, Tex.: Texas A&M University Press, 1989), 82.

SEAMAN DORIE MILLER

1. Langston Hughes. *Famous Negro Heroes of America* (New York: Dodd, Mead & Company, 1958), 186.
2. Ibid.

SECOND LIEUTENANT VERNON J. BAKER

1. "The War Hero from the Back of the Bus," *US News & World Report Online* (May 6, 1996), 2.

GENERAL DANIEL "CHAPPIE" JAMES JR.

1. *Current Biography 1976*, 197.
2. Ibid.

ADMIRAL SAMUEL L. GRAVELY JR.

1. "Guardian of the Pacific: Vice Admiral Samuel L. Gravely, Jr., Commands U.S. Third Fleet," *Ebony* (September 1977), 70.
2. Ibid., 72.
3. Ibid., 76.

GENERAL COLIN L. POWELL

1. Colin L. Powell. *My American Journey* (New York: Random House, 1995), 129.
2. Ibid., 557.

BRIGADIER GENERAL SHERIAN CADORIA

1. "The General Is a Lady," *Ebony* (December 1985), 146.

COLONEL GUION S. BLUFORD JR.

1. James Haskins. *Black Eagles: African Americans in Aviation* (New York: Scholastic 1995), 160.
2. Ibid., 162.

COMMANDER ROBERT O. GOODMAN JR.

1. "Goodman's Quest: The Best." *Newsday* (January 5, 1984).
2. D. Michael Cheers, "Lt. Robert Goodman: The Story Behind the Rescue," *Ebony* (March 1984), 161.

BIBLIOGRAPHY

BOOKS FOR ADULTS

Berlin, Ira, ed. *Freedom: A Documentary History of Emancipation 1861–1867. Series II: The Black Military Experience.* New York: Cambridge University Press, 1982.

Carroll, John M., ed. *The Black Military Experience in the American West.* New York: Liveright Publishing, 1971.

Franklin, John Hope. *George Washington Williams, A Biography.* Chicago: University of Chicago Press, 1985.

Gilmer, George R. *Sketches of First Settlers of Upper Georgia.* Baltimore, MD: Baltimore Genealogical Publishing Co., 1965; courtesy of Georgia Department of Archives and History, Atlanta.

Greene, Robert Ewell. *Black Defenders of America, 1775–1973.* Chicago: Johnson Publishing Co., 1974.

Haskins, Jim. *America's First Black Governor: Pinckney Benton Stewart Pinchback.* Trenton, N.J.: Africa World Press, 1996.

Kaplan, Sidney. *The Black Presence in the Era of the American Revolution, 1770–1800.* New York: New York Graphic Society, 1973.

Katz, William Loren. *The Black West: A Documentary and Pictorial History.* Garden City, N.Y.: Doubleday, 1971.

Lanning, Michael Lee. *The African-American Soldier: From Crispus Attucks to Colin Powell.* Secaucus, N.J.: Birch Lane Press, 1997.

McPherson, James M. *The Negro's Civil War.* New York: Ballantine Books, 1991.

Martin, Waldo E. Jr. *The Mind of Frederick Douglass.* Chapel Hill: University of North Carolina Press, 1984.

Moebs, Thomas Truxton. *Black Soldiers—Black Sailors—Black Ink.* Chesapeake Bay and Paris: Moebs Publishing, 1994.

Nalty, Bernard C. *Strength for the Fight: A History of Black Americans in the Military.* New York: The Free Press, 1986.

Powell, Colin L. *My American Journey.* New York: Random House, 1995.

Robinson, Wilhelmina. *Historical Afro-American Biographies.* Cornwells Heights, Penn.: The Publishers Agency, under the auspices of ASAALH, 1976.

Salzman, Jack, David Lionel Smith, and Cornel West, eds. *The Encyclopedia of African–American Culture and History.* New York: Simon & Schuster Macmillan, 1996.

Sandler, Stanley. *Segregated Skies: All-Black Combat Squadrons of WWII.* Washington, D.C.: Smithsonian Institution Press, 1992.

Schubert, Frank N. *On the Trail of the Buffalo Soldier: Biographies of African-Americans in the U.S. Army, 1866–1917.* Wilmington, Del.: Scholarly Resources, 1995.

Smith, Jessie Carney, ed. *Epic Lives: One Hundred Black Women Who Made a Difference.* Detroit: Visible Ink Press, 1993.

————. *Notable Black American Women.* Detroit: Gale Research, 1992.

Smythe, Mabel M., ed. *The Black American Reference Book.* Englewood Cliffs, N.J.: Prentice-Hall, 1976.

Sterling, Dorothy, ed. *We Are Your Sisters: Black Women in the Nineteenth Century.* New York: W.W. Norton, 1984.

Webster's American Military Biographies. Springfield, Mass.: G. & C. Merriam, 1978.

Williams, George Washington. *A History of the Negro Troops in the War of the Rebellion, 1861–1865.* New York: Kraus Reprint, 1969.

BOOKS FOR YOUNG READERS

Burchard, Peter. *"We'll Stand By the Union": Robert Gould Shaw and the Black 54th Massachusetts Regiment.* New York: Facts on File, 1993.

Chang, Ina. *A Separate Battle: Women and the Civil War.* New York: Lodestar Books, 1991.

Cooper, Michael L. *Hell Fighters: African Americans in World War I.* New York: Lodestar Books, 1997.

Cox, Clinton. *Undying Glory: The Story of the Massachusetts 54th Regiment.* New York: Scholastic, 1991.

Haskins, James. *Black Eagles: African Americans in Aviation.* New York: Scholastic, 1995.

————. *Get on Board: The Story of the Underground Railroad.* New York: Scholastic, 1993.

Hughes, Langston. *Famous Negro Heroes of America.* New York: Dodd, Mead & Company, 1958.

Littlefield, Daniel C. *Revolutionary Citizens: African Americans 1776–1804.* New York: Oxford University Press, 1997.

ARTICLES

Cheers, D. Michael. "Lt. Robert Goodman: The Story Behind the Rescue." *Ebony* (March 1984): 160–161ff.

Daniel "Chappie" James. *Current Biography 1976.*

"The General Is a Lady." *Ebony* (December 1985): 140ff.

"Goodman's Quest: The Best." *Newsday* (January 5, 1984).

"Guardian of the Pacific: Vice Admiral Samuel L. Gravely, Jr., Commands U.S. Third Fleet." *Ebony* (September 1977): 67–68ff.

"The War Hero from the Back of the Bus." *US News & World Report Online,* (May 6, 1996).

PICTURE CREDITS

Page 8: courtesy of the Yale University Art Gallery, New Haven, Conn.; page 12: courtesy of the Library of Congress, Washington, D.C.; page 13: courtesy of the Virginia Historical Society, Richmond; page 15: Museum of Art/Rhode Island School of Design, Providence; page 20: public domain; page 25: courtesy of the Library of Congress, Washington, D.C.; page 28: The UT Institute of Texan Cultures at San Antonio, courtesy of Texas Southern University; page 34: courtesy of the National Portrait Gallery, Smithsonian Institution/Art Resource, New York; pages 37 and 40: courtesy of the Library of Congress, Washington, D.C.; page 46: courtesy of Culver Pictures, Inc.; page 49: courtesy of Moorland-Spingarn Research Center, Howard University, Washington, D.C.; page 52: courtesy of the Library of Congress, Washington, D.C.; page 58: public domain; pages 61 and 64: courtesy of the Library of Congress, Washington, D.C.; page 66: courtesy of the Minnesota Historical Society, St. Paul; page 68: courtesy of Moorland-Spingarn Research Center, Howard University, Washington, D.C.; page 70: courtesy of National Archives, Washington, D.C.; page 72: courtesy of Moorland-Spingarn Research Center, Howard University, Washington, D.C.; page 80: courtesy of the Library of Congress, Washington, D.C., page 83: courtesy of the Montana Historical Society, Helena; page 86: courtesy of National Archives, Washington, D.C.; page 88: courtesy of the Library of Congress, Washington, D.C.; pages 93, 98, and 100; courtesy of National Archives, Washington, D.C.; page 104: courtesy of the Smithsonian Institution, Washington, D.C.; page 107: courtesy of the National Air and Space Museum; page 108: courtesy of the U.S. Air Force; pages 111 and 116; courtesy of National Archives, Washington D.C.; page 120: courtesy of the National Archives, Washington, D.C.; page 126: courtesy of the U.S. Air Force; page 131: courtesy of the U.S. Navy; page 133: courtesy of the Library of Congress, Washington, D.C.; page 136: courtesy of Photographs and Prints Div., Schomburg Center for Research in Black Culture, The New York Public Library/Astor, Lenox and Tilden Foundations; page 140: courtesy of the U.S. Army; page 143: courtesy of Reuters/Corbis-Bettmann; page 148: courtesy of the U.S. Army; page 152: courtesy of the National Aeronautics and Space Administration (NASA), Washington, D.C.; page 158: courtesy of the U.S. Air Force.

INDEX

Qui Nhom Support Command (South Vietnam), 149

Texas Revolution, 29–30
Third Division, Eighteenth Army
    Troops, 65
Thirteenth Cavalry, 89
Thirty-third Tactical Fighter Wing,
    127–28
Thomas, Benjamin, 19
332d Fighter Group, 96, 107, 109
Tillman, Lieutenant B. R., 88
Tompkins, Major Frank, 89
trench, defined, 99
Truman, President Harry S., 3, 95, 109,
    127
Trumbull, John, 9
Tubman, Harriet, **45–50**
Tuskegee Airmen, 3, 106, 107, 125, 127
Tuskegee Institute, 89, 95, 103, 125
Twenty-fifth Army Corps, 73
Twenty-fifth Infantry Regiment, 121
Twenty-seventh Infantry, 74

Underground Railroad, 47, 48
United Nations, 145
United States Coast Guard, 57
United States Military Academy at
    West Point. *See* West Point
United States Revenue Cutter Service,
    57, 59
Upson, Stephen, 13
U.S. Colored Troops, 73
U.S. Naval Reserve, 130
U.S. Navy, 59, 62, 118, 132, 134
USS *Falgout* (ship), 134
USS *Iowa* (ship), 132
USS *Jouett* (ship), 134
USS *Liscome Bay* (ship), 118
USS *Miller* (ship), 118
USS *PC-1264* (sub-chaser), 132
USS *Revenge* (ship), 26
USS *Theodore E. Chandler* (ship), 134
USS *Toledo* (ship), 134
USS *West Virginia* (ship), 115
Utah (ship), 117

Van Buren, President Martin, 26
Vashon, Captain George, 26

Vashon, Seaman John Bathan, **24–26**
Vietnam Veterans Memorial, 143
Vietnam War, 3, 127–28, 141–42, 149,
    153–54
Villa, Francisco "Pancho," 89
Vogelsang, Lieutenant Peter, **39–44**

War Department, 66, 112
Warmoth, Governor Henry Clay, 55
War of 1812, 1, 24–26, 27
Washington, Booker T., 89
Washington, President George, 9, 16, 26
Webb, Captain George, 21
Weinberger, Caspar, 143
West Point
    Davis, Benjamin O. Jr., 105
    Davis, Benjamin O. Sr., 94
    Flipper, Henry Ossian, 79, 81, 82
    Young, Charles A., 85, 87, 94
White House Fellows, 142
Wilberforce University, 87, 88, 95, 110,
    114
Wilder, Governor L. Douglas, 55
Williams, Sergeant George Washing-
    ton, 71–75
Women Accepted for Voluntary Emer-
    gency Service (WAVE), 112
Women's Army Corps (WAC), 3, 110,
    112
Women's Auxiliary Corps (WAAC),
    110, 112–13
World War I, 2
    Davis, Benjamin O. Sr., 96
    Johnson, Henry, 97, 99–100
    victory march, 100
World War II, 2–3, 125
    Baker, Vernon J., 121–23
    Davis, Benjamin O. Jr., 106–8
    Davis, Benjamin O. Sr., 96
    Gravely, Samuel L. Jr., 130, 132
    Miller, Dorie, 117–18
    Pearl Harbor, Japanese bombing of,
        106, 115, 117, 121

Young, Colonel Charles A., 85–91, 94,
    105